To

_____

From

_____

On this date

_____

BRAVE GIRLS
BIBLE STORIES

Brave Girls Bible Stories

© 2014 by Thomas Nelson

Written by Jennifer Gerelds

Illustrations by Aleksey and Olga Ivanov

Published in Nashville, Tennessee, by Tommy Nelson. Tommy Nelson is an imprint of Thomas Nelson. Thomas Nelson is a registered trademark of HarperCollins Christian Publishing, Inc.

Tommy Nelson titles may be purchased in bulk for educational, business, fund-raising, or sales promotional use. For information, please e-mail SpecialMarkets@ThomasNelson.com.

Unless otherwise noted, Scripture quotations are from the International Children's Bible®. © 1986, 1988, 1999 by Thomas Nelson. All rights reserved.

Scripture quotations noted NKJV are from THE NEW KING JAMES VERSION. © 1982 by Thomas Nelson. Used by permission. All rights reserved.

ISBN: 978-0-529-10898-2

Library of Congress Cataloging-in-Publication Data is on file.

18 19 DSC 10 9 8 7

Printed in China
www.thomasnelson.com

mfr: DSC / Shenzhen, China / September 2018 / PO# 9516056

Celebrating Great Women of the Bible

BRAVE GIRLS
BIBLE STORIES

Written by
JENNIFER GERELDS

Illustrated by
Aleksey & Olga Ivanov

A Division of Thomas Nelson Publishers

Table of Contents

Introduction

We Have tHis Hope,
so we aRe veRy bRave.

2 CoRintHians 3:12

If you had to name the top five bravest people you know, who would make the list? Maybe your mom or dad? A pastor? A teacher? A friend? *You?*

Chances are, you've probably never thought of yourself as brave. After all, it's not likely that you've rescued someone from a burning building or saved someone from drowning (you know, all those heroic acts you've seen someone do on TV that everyone calls "brave"). No, you are just you, doing your school thing, going to church, and having fun with hobbies and friends. *No real need for bravery around here,* you might think.

Well, that's what the girls in our church youth group thought at first too. Hope, Honor, Glory, Faith, and Gracie—the girls you'll meet in the next few pages—didn't see anything really spectacular about their lives. A word like *bravery* was supposed to be saved for big-time heroes, not small-town, ordinary girls, right?

So when they all began studying how God used ordinary girls in the Bible to accomplish amazing things for His kingdom, they were blown away. Story after story showed how God worked incredible wonders whenever His girls simply followed His lead. It didn't take sensational abilities or outrageous events—just simple faith from regular people trusting an extraordinary God to do miraculous things.

Our youth group girls are all super excited to tell you what God has shown them about His brave Bible girls and the really cool ways He's helping them to be brave for God at school, at home, in their sports, with their friends—pretty much everywhere. It seems God didn't just make girls brave back then. He's still at it today. And now He's calling you. Ready for some action? Be brave and turn the page. It's time to get going!

And remember: it's His love that makes us strong.

Meet the Brave Girls

Hope

Ready for a game of football? Yeah, I know I'm a girl. And girls aren't supposed to play football, right? Well, you haven't seen me with my brothers. Every Saturday afternoon we're out in the yard playing flag football with our neighbors. And if it isn't football, it's soccer or softball. We even have a volleyball net! I guess that's one advantage to living on a farm outside of town—plenty of room to play hard.

I actually have a girly side to me that likes to dress up and be pretty and all that stuff. But give me a pair of broken-in jeans, a T-shirt, and a good group of friends, and I'm happier than a homecoming queen.

I guess you could say nothing in my life is all that fancy. Farm life just isn't that way. But I have a terrific family. I'm the oldest, and my two younger brothers are twins my parents adopted from the Ukraine when they were two years old. I love those guys, even though they bother me sometimes. We all work together around the farm and around our church. We help out with the local charity too because we can't get over how good God has been to us. And sharing His hope with others? Well, it beats football any day.

I do admit that I have a challenge I don't like to talk about—reading. I do okay in school for the most part. But when I read, the letters get mixed up, and sometimes it looks like another language to me. They call it dyslexia. I call it embarrassing. But I do my best to remember that God can help me tackle this challenge. And He's where I'm learning to put my—you guessed it—hope!

Glory

If you could be anywhere in the world right now, where would you be? I'm kind of torn. Half of me would want to be on a high mountain somewhere, enjoying a beautiful sunset. Or maybe the beach, looking out across the sparkling waters. But the other half of me would be just as wonderstruck walking down the streets of New York City with my mom and sisters, shopping for all the latest fashions! I mean, you can never have enough boots, right? Or scarves and earrings and nail polish to match?

Yes, I know it might sound weird, but there is a common thread to everything I love: beauty! I love beauty wherever I see it. In this awesome world God created, in a gorgeous dress in a store window, and in the great hugs I get from my friends. I think God's beauty is everywhere—you just have to look for it.

Lately, I've had to look a little harder. Life at home wasn't so pretty, and just last summer my parents got divorced. For a while, I got really mad at God and forgot about the good in the world. But then my friends from the youth group started writing me encouraging notes and inviting me over. Their love and friendship was, well, beautiful—and it got me noticing all the other amazing ways God shows His love to me. I've started to see how God can take even the ugly, hard things in life and turn them into something good. I'm working on forgiving my parents and praying that God will use me to encourage other girls like me. You know, God can take even the messiest of situations and use them for His glory!

Honor

My friends say that wherever there's a challenge, I'm the one to take it! Maybe that's why I always pick up stray animals and bring them home. I love to care for my furry friends and figure out how to make them better. I'm always going to the library to find new books to help me in my animal rescue mission! In fact, I love to read books in general. Last summer I started volunteering at the library so that I could help other kids learn to love books too.

But my biggest challenge lately hasn't been at the library or with my five pets. It's been at school. Studying has always been easy for me, and I was thrilled when the principal said I could skip a grade. But I had a really hard time fitting in with the older kids. They didn't seem impressed with my intelligence, so at first I tried dressing and talking more like they did, even though I knew it didn't honor God. That didn't work either.

I just ended up feeling guilty and more out-of-place than ever. Turns out they weren't the kind of friends I needed anyway. It's a good thing God has given me an awesome youth group. My leader and friends there have helped me remember who God says I am.

So who am I, really? You could say I'm God's girl, even though I don't *always* act like it. But I am learning how to honor Him more. And one day I hope to take all the abilities God has given me and use them, maybe to become a veterinarian or zoologist or something. Whatever I do, though, one thing's for sure: I want it all to honor God.

GRacie

Let's just say it's all by God's grace that I'm here. And I'm not just saying that because of my name. If it had been left up to me, I'd still be in my old hometown of Perkasie, Pennsylvania. We're talking beautiful green hills and parks on every street corner. I was born there, and I knew everybody (and everybody knew me) . . .

And then we moved. I thought life was over. I wanted my old friends and old world back, and I was pretty stubborn and loud about it.

In my hometown, my family and I didn't talk about God much. But once we moved here, we started going to this church, and there were some girls in the youth group who were . . . nice. More than nice, really. They were cool. They liked to do fun stuff and all, but they also weren't afraid to talk about things that matter—like what we're supposed to do with our lives. I used to ask myself that question sometimes, like when I was walking through the woods by my house or listening to my music. These girls were able to show me the answer in the Bible. I always knew there had to be a God who made all those beautiful things. Now I'm beginning to know who He is, thanks to God Himself, those girls, my church, and, yes, even my parents who moved me here.

Wanna know something else kind of funny? The only time I ever sang back in Pennsylvania was in my shower at home. I loved it, but I was afraid to sing in public. Now I'm in the choir at church, and I'm singing about God to anybody who'll listen!

Faith

Have you ever known anybody who is homeschooled? If you haven't, now you do! My sister and I have been homeschooled all our lives. I miss my friends, but I still love learning at home because I have more time—to finish my work, to hang out, and to think. I've even used that time to start reading the Bible on my own because I really want to make God happy.

But to tell the truth, I tend to try to please more than just God. I want everyone to like what I do, which has made me quite a perfectionist. Even though my name is Faith, I think a better name right now would be "Worry" because I'm always worried that I'm going to disappoint someone, including myself. The only time I get away from those thoughts is when I'm painting, my favorite hobby. Fortunately, I find lots of time for that, which is starting to pay off. I've been asked to help the younger kids with their art projects at camp this year, and I've even won some local art contests!

The girls in the youth group are helping me too, and I love spending time with them. They remind me that God already knows all about my mess ups and sins but loves me anyway. I guess I'm learning that my faith is not a bunch of "dos and don'ts." It's about a relationship with God, who knows the *real* me, and He is working on me to make me more like Him. That's what real faith is all about—believing that God loves me, forgives me, and sees me as His very own work of art, no matter what!

The Youth Group

If God had thought we worked better alone, He wouldn't have invited so many people into His family. We need each other! Just like a body works best when all its parts are connected, God's family is the strongest when all His kids work and worship together.

But a funny thing often happens with a big group of people who spend a lot of time together. The people start to look the same. They dress the same, talk the same, and only welcome other people who, well, are just like them. Now, can you imagine if, on your body, your nose decided to be an eye instead? And then, out of peer pressure, your ear became an eye, then your hands, and . . . you get the picture. You'd have a body of eyes without any ability to move, feel, taste, touch, or smell. Plus, you'd creep a lot of people out.

Each one of us has a special way to honor God and help others see Him in ways the rest of us can't on our own. But together, we're even stronger—which is a great part of God's plan.

That's what our youth group is all about: learning how to work together to know God better and to tell other people about Him too. We meet every week to talk, to learn what God is saying to us in the Bible, and to pray about anything and everything—together, the way God's family was meant to be. Want to join us?

OLD TESTAMENT

His Love
Makes Us
Strong

Picture Perfect

Genesis 1–4:1

> We know that in everything God works for the good of those who love him.
>
> Romans 8:28

THE GARDEN OF EDEN WAS ONE PERFECT GARDEN. Out of absolutely nothing, God created the most amazing universe. Incredible animals and colors and sounds and smells. Everything was picture-perfect and ran right on time, in just the right way, exactly how I wish life would be.

But life isn't perfect anymore, is it? No matter how hard I try, I just can't get everything to work out like I planned! That's because sin entered God's perfect world. God created the world's first people, Adam and Eve, in His own image. They got to live in that beautiful garden and have a perfect relationship with God! But then Eve believed Satan instead of God and talked Adam into disobeying God too. Suddenly, it was like someone poured dark ink over the beautiful picture God had made. Life seemed ruined.

My little sister accidentally poured paint over one of my best paintings one time, so I can kind of imagine how God must have felt. But God had an awesome way of painting over Adam and Eve's sins with the perfect solution.

Before Eve entered the scene, God had already been busy. With His word, He made the universe burst into being. On the first day, He made day and night. On day two came the the sky. He zeroed in on the earth for day three and made oceans and mountains, forests and deserts. He filled the pastures with green grass and a rainbow of flowers. On the fourth day, the sun, moon, and stars first appeared in the sky.

And then came the creatures! On day five, birds were flying through the skies and fish were diving in the oceans. And on the sixth day, animals began crawling and running and leaping across the grass. But God had something even more amazing to make . . . people! In His own image, God made Adam from the dirt of the ground and breathed life into him. God made Eve next, from Adam's own rib when he was in a deep sleep.

Imagine what Eve saw when her eyes first fluttered open. There was Adam, the first man God had made. Then she looked around and saw all the beauty in the garden of Eden. It must have been awesome. I bet it took her breath away!

Eve, the first woman ever created, was perfect—just like the creation around her. So what happened? Why isn't our world like God made it in the beginning?

Although the garden was filled with yummy fruit trees to eat from, God had warned Adam and Eve that they would die if they ate from one of the trees in the center of the garden, the tree of the knowledge of good and evil. God gave them the chance to make choices, good or bad.

Satan, God's enemy, decided that forbidden tree was the perfect place to trick Eve. So, in the form of a snake, Satan slithered to the tree and told Eve a lie. "You won't die like God said if you eat this," Satan said. "You'll just become smart like God."

This fruit does look really good, Eve thought. So she ate the forbidden fruit and gave some to Adam. Then everything changed. Immediately, she and Adam were ashamed they had no clothes on, so they sewed fig leaves together to cover up. Then they hid when they heard God coming. Not looking very brave at all, Eve was shaking, scared at what God would do when He saw the mess she had made.

Adam and Eve's disobedience had some big consequences. Death and sadness and pain entered the world, hurting all of creation. Adam and Eve had to leave the garden, and the perfect place wasn't perfect anymore.

The good thing is God didn't leave Adam and Eve—He loved them too much, and He had a plan. Many, many years later, God sent His own Son, Jesus, to earth. As God and man, Jesus would live the perfect life that no one else could. Then He would die to cover Eve's sins—and mine, and yours, and everyone else's who trusts Him! Better still, He would rise from the dead. He fought sin and won!

Wow! I can't imagine what all Eve must have felt. I have a hard enough time when I lose my temper or say something mean to my sister. Sometimes I get so frustrated with myself that I don't want to try to do things right anymore.

I guess that's why I think Eve was so brave. She made a horrible decision that hurt her, Adam, and the rest of the world. But Eve kept going, and God helped her!

Eve reminds us that no sin or bad choice is too big for God to cover. His love outshines our not-so-good days, and even though we're not perfect, He promises us forgiveness through someone who is perfect—Jesus! I'm so glad we belong to a God like that.

Lord, help me have faith that You will always love me, forgive me, and take care of me. Amen.

The Life Saver

Genesis 6–9

The Lord God helps me. So I will not be ashamed. I will be determined. I know I will not be disgraced.

Isaiah 50:7

I'M SURE IT WAS TOUGH FOR NOAH AND ALL. I mean, everybody around him was doing wrong things and making bad decisions. I bet nobody was like, "Hey, Noah, I think you're really smart for building a big boat on dry land with no water in sight." I bet the jokes got pretty old in the years it took to build that giant ark.

But I think it also had to be rough for Noah's wife. She had to trust that God was able to lead her through her husband, and she had to stand by Noah even when others thought he was nuts. And don't you know the ladies around town whispered when she walked down the street!

Some historians think Noah's wife might have been named Emzara, but the Bible doesn't let us know for sure. But we *do* know she was brave enough to ignore the God-haters around her and do what was right instead. She got in the boat without a raindrop in sight.

Imagine living in a place where you were scared to walk out your front door. That's how it was for Noah and his family. Everyone around them was doing horrible things. Violence was everywhere. I bet it was like what we hear in the news sometimes about people getting robbed and killed. But those days were worse—*everyone's* thoughts were filled with evil. Everyone, that is, except Noah and his family.

Now, I don't know why Noah was a good man when no one else was. But he decided to stick with God and stay away from everybody else. Boy, did God notice! God had enough of the violence and evil. He told Noah, "People have made the earth full of violence. So I will destroy all people on the earth."

But God had a very strange plan to save Noah and his family, along with every species of animal. He told Noah to build a boat—in the middle of a very dry land. Not a small boat that he could hide from everybody. God wanted a huge ark that could hold all those animals, their food, and Noah's family of eight (that would be Noah and his wife, their three sons, and their sons' wives).

The Bible stays quiet about what Noah's wife had to say about all this. But we do know she went right onto that ark with all those loud and smelly animals without a single recorded temper tantrum—I know I could not have done that. I'm sure I would've had a major fit!

Then you know what happened? Nothing. Nada. I mean, I would have called it quits right then, but Noah and his wife kept trusting God. Day one went by. Then two. Three. Four. Five. Six. Are you kidding me? No! But on day seven, their obedience paid off when they saw that God was right. Water poured from the sky and up from the ground, flooding the entire earth until the world was covered. Can you imagine? Every person and every creature that was not on the boat died.

Guess how long Noah's family was on the ark? Well, the Bible says Noah was 600 years old when the flood began, and he was 601 when the land dried and they got to get out. I guess you can do the math. That's a long time to be on a boat with all those animals. But do you know what Noah and his wife and family did first thing when they got off? They offered a sacrifice to God, thanking Him for taking care of them. God answered with a rainbow in the sky and a promise to never again destroy the entire earth with a flood .

Noah's wife must have been tough. She chose to go against the crowd and the wrong things they were doing. She listened to Noah, and to God, instead. Her bravery and obedience saved her life.

Just like Noah's wife showed her trust in God by obeying and entering the ark, you can show you trust God when you obey His Word. I know it's hard to follow God when no one else is. So remember Noah's wife when you're getting tired of doing what's right. Trust in God, obey, and wait for Him. You've got a rainbow of blessings ahead if you do.

Lord, I want to stick with You no matter what others are doing. Help me be like Noah's wife, who trusted and obeyed! Amen.

Beautiful Timing
Genesis 12-21

Your beauty should come from within you—
the beauty of a gentle and quiet spirit.
This beauty will never disappear, and
it is worth very much to God. It was
the same with the holy
women who lived long
ago and followed God.

1 Peter 3:4-5

CAN YOU IMAGINE BEING SO BEAUTIFUL THAT HEADS TURNED WHEN YOU WALKED BY? With power like that, you'd think you could have whatever you wanted.

But let me introduce you to Sarah, formerly known as Sarai, wife of the famous Abraham, formerly known as Abram—wow, did you follow that? She lived thousands of years ago, so I don't know exactly what she looked like. But the Bible tells us one thing for sure: she was drop-dead gorgeous! And it wasn't just her husband who noticed either. It sounds like just about every place she went, people thought she was pretty awesome.

But brave Sarah didn't just shine because of her outward beauty. You see, beauty—as great as it may seem—doesn't last. We all go gray and get wrinkles as we age, just like Sarah did. But God grew a timeless beauty in her heart that still shines when we tell her story. God may have made Sarah pretty on the outside, but the beautiful transformation that happened in her heart is the real story to tell.

First, it was the move. Abram, Sarai's husband, wanted her to pack her things and go with him to some new place they'd never been, far away from her home and all she loved. I don't know about you, but I sure wouldn't have wanted to obey.

But Sarai did. They traveled with Abram's nephew and their family and some servants and animals. Why were they going? Because God told Abram that He had reserved a special place just for him. He was going to need a lot of land because God was going to bless him by making him the father of many nations. What a promise! I'm sure that news helped Sarai keep going when the going got tough.

When Abram and Sarai moved to Egypt, Pharaoh noticed Sarai's beauty and wanted to marry her. Abram got scared. *If the pharaoh knows that I'm her husband*, he thought, *he might kill me to get to her.* So he told Sarai his not-so-brilliant idea: "Tell them you are my sister." Yikes! Poor Sarai ended up away from her husband and in the Egyptian king's palace. Fortunately, God was not okay with this ridiculousness and stepped in to save Sarai and get her back where she belonged: with Abram.

Not long after that, Abram and Sarai made it to Canaan, and God appeared to Abram again to tell him that he was going to have a very blessed son one day. Through that son, a whole nation would grow—a nation so huge that there would be more people than there were stars in the sky! Now that's my kind of kingdom. The more people, the better—think of how many *more* shenanigans you could have with *more* people!

Only there was one little problem. As beautiful as Sarai was, she wasn't able to have babies. In fact, at this point, Sarai was getting old—too old. Even though God had taken care of her in the past, this time she didn't believe Him, and she got tired of waiting for Him to do something. So she gave her maid Hagar to Abram to be like a wife who could have a baby for Sarai. Hagar had a baby boy, but he wasn't the one God had promised Abram. Instead, God appeared to Abram again to tell him that Sarai and Abram would still have a son—even though Abram was almost one hundred years old, and Sarai was ninety! To prepare them for the blessing ahead, God changed their names to Abraham and Sarah. They would become the parents of a great nation that belonged to God.

A while later, Sarah got to hear the news for herself. When the Lord appeared to Abraham again and told him Sarah would have a son by this time next year, Sarah was listening from behind. Wrinkled and no longer the young beauty she had been, Sarah laughed to herself and said, "My husband and I are too old to have a baby!" But the Lord asked Abraham, "Why did Sarah laugh? Is anything too hard for the Lord?"

The answer was a major "no!" Within the year, Sarah had given birth to a baby boy, Isaac, who became the father of Jacob. And Jacob was the father of God's great nation—Israel.

Glory says . . .

I love beautiful things, and I think it's awesome that God chose someone gorgeous like Sarah to be the mother of Israel. But Sarah was a lot more than just a pretty face. She was a real person who lived a hard life and learned how important it is to trust God in the middle of it.

But why do you think God waited so long to give Sarah her son? Isaac wasn't born when Sarah was young and beautiful but when Sarah was old and wrinkled. If you ask me, I say God's answer is about time, trust, and true beauty. *Time*, because God works at His pace, not ours. *Trust*, because we need to believe God's promises. And *true beauty* happens not when we're looking good on the outside but when we wait for God to work it inside us.

Sarah's story reminds me of the beautiful truth: nothing is too hard for the Lord! He can do whatever He wants through me—and you. He has a plan for each of us that's bigger and better than we can imagine. Like Sarah, we just need to wait for Him!

Lord, thank You that nothing is too hard for You. You make everything beautiful and right in its time.

The Well Wisher

Genesis 24

"The master answered, 'You did well. You are a good servant who can be trusted. You did well with small things. So I will let you care for much greater things. Come and share my happiness with me.'"

Matthew 25:21

DID YOU KNOW THAT A CAMEL CAN DRINK UP TO TWENTY-FIVE GALLONS OF WATER AT ONE TIME? I know, right? It's amazing! They don't store it in their hump either, like lots of people think. The water goes into their bloodstream, where they can store it and slowly use it as they need it over long desert walks... like the one Abraham's servant took, along with ten of his master's camels. He was going on a long trip to find a wife for Isaac. His young bride turned out to be Rebekah, one of my favorite Bible brave girls.

t had been an ordinary day for Rebekah. She was heading to the well right outside the city to draw water for her family, which is what women did in those days. That day, though, a man was seated beside the well—a man who had ten camels. Curiously, the man ran up to her and asked, "Please let me drink a little water from your pitcher." Rebekah quickly lowered her jar and offered it to him, not having any idea that mere moments before, the same man had been praying for her! As he drank, Rebekah offered to get water from the well for his camels too.

Now stop for a minute. Remember how much water I said a camel could drink? That's right: up to twenty-five gallons each. How many camels did the man have? Ten! We don't know how much water Rebekah actually got from the well, but those camels could have been thirsty for as much as 250 gallons of water. Wow!

Who was this man who settled back and watched Rebekah give water to all of his camels?

The man was in town on a mission. Abraham had sent him to his homeland to find a wife for Abraham's son, Isaac. The girl had to be from a certain family, and she couldn't have been married before. Not only that, but she'd have to be willing to leave her own family to travel back with a man she didn't know to marry Isaac, whom she had never met.

So Abraham's servant traveled to his master's homeland, and he prayed. He asked God to find the right girl and bring her to him. He said to God, "Let it be that the young woman to whom I say, 'Please let down your pitcher that I may drink,' and she says, 'Drink, and I will also give your camels a drink'—let her be the one!" He hadn't even finished praying when Rebekah arrived and said those special words.

Abraham's servant knew Rebekah was God's choice for a wife for Isaac. The servant brought out a nose ring (hey, it was normal in those days) and two heavy gold bracelets. Then he asked Rebekah whose daughter she was.

And you guessed it: she was from the right family. Rebekah saw that God had chosen her, so she chose to trust Him back. She went with the servant to Canaan, married Isaac, and became the mother of Jacob, an important man in Israel's history.

Honor says . . .

I can relate to Rebekah. Every day I have to lug water out to my horse and my other pets. In fact, I have a lot of chores I have to do every day. They can get pretty tiring, and sometimes I don't even want to do them.

But then I think of Rebekah. What if she had been tired that day and hadn't offered to give water to the servant? And then to all those camels! She must have worked so hard to serve, but God had a major reward waiting for her at the end of all her effort.

Sometimes following God in the little things is hard. We get tired of doing homework, and we don't want to do chores. But Rebekah shows us that when we give our very best each and every moment, we honor God. When we are faithful in the small things, God can use us in some very big ways. Like Rebekah, we have to be brave and trust God to lead us every step of the way!

Lord, help me be like Rebekah and be faithful to do my best for You, even in the small things. Amen.

The Game Plan

Genesis 29-30

You can get the horses ready for battle. But it is the Lord who gives the victory.

Proverbs 21:31

ALL I NEED IS A BALL OR A RACQUET, A FEW FRIENDS, AND I'M SET. In no time at all, I'll get a good game of whatever-you-like underway. I think life's just a little better with some friendly competition.

Maybe that's why I like sports so much. If you know the rules, you can generally play the game and have some fun with it. But relationships—well, that's a whole different ballgame. It seems like people don't play by the same set of rules. Can you imagine if there were a thousand different ways to play soccer? Crazy, I know!

That's the kind of game Rachel and Leah played against each other in this Bible story, and it was hard for both of them. But I like their story because in the end they had to learn that God makes the rules, and life is better when we play by those rules and trust Him. Everybody wins that way.

Boys. They sure can mess with a girl's brain. One day when Rachel was walking to the well to water her sheep, she saw Jacob for the first time. Like a real gentleman, Jacob moved a heavy stone away from the well. And then he kissed her. I guess you could say it was love at first sight.

Jacob asked Rachel's father, Laban, for his permission to marry Rachel. Laban was a businessman—the not-so-honest kind. But he agreed to let Jacob marry Rachel if Jacob worked for him for seven years first.

Yes, seven years. That's 2,555 days of work! Jacob must have loved Rachel so much because he agreed. But when the wedding day finally arrived, Laban broke the rules of the game. He switched out the players, so to speak, and gave Leah, his older daughter, to Jacob instead.

But Jacob didn't want Leah—he wanted Rachel! Laban made him agree to work *another* seven years so he could marry Rachel too. Jacob agreed, and after seven years Jacob and Rachel tied the knot.

Now, I would tell the ref at this point that too many players were on the field because two wives is definitely one too many. But things were different back then, and the sisters had to learn to live together. But poor Leah! She wasn't pretty like Rachel, and her husband didn't love her like he loved her sister. So God comforted Leah by giving her lots of children. She gave each one a special name that showed she knew that God was watching her, and that even if her husband didn't care for her, God did.

But then Rachel got upset. Compared to Leah, she was losing the baby race, and she didn't like the way this game was headed. She wanted children too! But God told her no for a while. In the last few minutes of the game, Rachel had two sons. All in God's time and plan, Leah and Rachel became an important part of giving birth to God's special people: the twelve tribes of Israel.

Hope says . . .

At first glance, neither Leah nor Rachel looks particularly brave.

But on second glance, you see true grit: Leah, who pressed on in spite of being rejected by her husband, and Rachel, who persevered through watching her sister marry the man who loved her and then waiting while she tried to have babies. In the end, God blessed them both with children and an honored place in Israel's family tree.

Both of these ladies remind me that God is working a far better game plan for my life than I can often understand. That's what He's promised to do for all of us who love Him!

Lord, help me hope in You instead of trying to work things out the way I want. Amen.

The Fantastic Four

Exodus 1-2

"I tell you the truth. If your faith
is as big as a mustard seed,
you can say to this mountain,
'Move from here to there.'
And the mountain will move. All
things will be possible for you."

Matthew 17:20

MOSES IS ONE OF THE MOST FAMOUS BIBLE GUYS EVER.
It's not every day that a baby gets put in a basket to
float on a river, straight into the arms of an unsuspect-
ing princess, and then gets to grow up in an Egyptian
palace...or is spoken to by God through a burning bush!

And that's just the beginning of an amazing story. But what many people don't
notice—at least, not right away—are all the supporting stars in Moses' sensational
story. That baby didn't get into that basket by accident! No, it was part of a plan God
was working out through the lives of four faith-filled women.

So naturally, I want to fill you in on how the bravery of these girls of God saved not
only a little boy from certain death, but also the entire nation of Israel in the long run.
I'll start by painting a picture for you of just how bad things had gotten in Egypt...

magine a very angry pharaoh. (That's one of those Egyptian kings who looked like King Tut; you might have seen them in books.) He had just gotten word that the Israelite crowd in his kingdom was growing even bigger, and he wanted them stopped.

"Look!" he cried. "There are too many Israelites! And they are too strong for us to handle! We must make plans against them." So the pharaoh started thinking of ways to control the unwanted Israelites . . . mean ways.

What could he do? Well, he could make life for the Israelites miserable, so that's exactly what he did. He ordered the Egyptians to treat God's people harshly by beating them and giving them more work than they could possibly finish. He hoped it would make them so tired and frustrated that they'd stop having so many babies and growing more powerful.

But Pharaoh's plan backfired. God made His people multiply even faster. And Pharaoh got madder than ever. So he commanded two women to come before his throne. Their names were Shiphrah and Puah, and they were the midwives who helped the Hebrew babies to be born.

I picture Pharaoh looking at Shiphrah and Puah with his eyebrows down and a scowl on his face. "When you are helping the Hebrew women give birth to their babies, watch!"

It was so quiet you could hear a pin drop. Then came the horrible command: "If the baby is a girl, let the baby live. But if it is a boy, kill it!"

Gasp! Can you imagine? What kind of terrible person would order such a thing? Pharaoh, that's who. And he was powerful enough to make it happen. If Shiphrah and Puah didn't obey, they could be killed.

But these brave women of God didn't blink an eye. Shiphrah and Puah marched out of Pharaoh's palace and went right on helping those Hebrew women have their babies, boys and girls alike. In fact, God was good to them, gave them families of their own, and blessed their work. They were probably at the home of a woman named Jochebed when she gave birth to Moses—a beautiful, healthy Hebrew boy.

I'm sure it was a very happy moment, but all the women must have known they were in danger for disobeying Pharaoh's orders. They had let baby Moses live, but he was still in danger too. For three months, mama Jochebed hid baby Moses from the Egyptian soldiers who would have killed him. But babies do grow, and she couldn't hide him forever. What on earth was she going to do?

The rule was that every baby boy was supposed to be thrown into the Nile River. So Jochebed decided to obey, but with one big twist: she covered a basket with tar so that it would float and no water could get inside. Then she gently put baby Moses inside and set the basket in the tall grass of the Nile River.

Moses' sister, Miriam, watched quietly from a distance. *I wonder what's going to happen?* she thought.

Soon, Pharaoh's daughter, the princess, came to the river to bathe. It didn't take long for her to spot the basket floating nearby, so she summoned a servant to fetch it for her. She opened the basket and exclaimed, "This is one of the Hebrew babies!" I bet his sad cries were already melting her heart.

Miriam decided that helping her baby brother was worth the risk of getting caught. She bravely approached the princess. "Would you like me to find a Hebrew woman to take care of the baby for you?" she asked, as if she'd have to look long and hard to find one.

"Yes, please," replied the princess. Immediately, Miriam ran to her mother, Jochebed, and brought her to the princess.

"Take this baby and nurse him for me," the princess told Jochebed. "I will pay you."

Can you believe it? Moses' own mother not only got to keep her son alive and at home with her, but now she was also going to get paid to do it! I wonder if God was laughing over all the fun ways He was working His miraculous plan for His people? Only He knew Moses would grow up being trained in Pharaoh's palace, so that he could return years later to save all the Hebrew people from Pharaoh's evil rule.

Faith says . . .

Shiphrah, Puah, Jochebed, and Miriam each took big risks to do the right thing. Whenever I am faced with impossible situations, I like to remember this group of God-honoring ladies. God knew what was going on in each of their lives and gave each lady exactly what she needed at just the right time. That's the kind of thing that always happens when you are trusting God to take care of you. These ladies' stories remind me that nothing is impossible with God because He has the power to do whatever He pleases! My job is to have faith that God will take care of me and to show my faith by obeying what He tells me to do.

Lord, nothing is too hard for You. Please give me the faith I need to obey and follow You. Amen.

Pray that when I preach the Good News I will speak without fear, as I should.

Ephesians 6:20

SOMETHING INTERESTING HAPPENED TODAY AT SCHOOL. Gracie, one of my new friends from youth group, got her history paper back, and she looked upset. I asked her what was wrong, and she told me her teacher had counted off several points on her paper because she had talked too much about God in it. Gracie had written about how many of the men who founded America were Christians, but her teacher didn't agree.

I started to get mad at her teacher, but then I thought about this short-but-cool Bible story about Zelophehad's daughters and how they handled things when justice wasn't being served. It gave me an idea of how I could help Gracie and honor God too.

Have your parents ever promised to take you some place really special, like the beach or Disney World? Didn't it feel like forever for that day to arrive? I imagine that times a million must have been how the Israelites felt when they finally got to go into the land God promised them. They followed Moses out of Egypt, but because of their disobedience, they wandered in the desert for forty years! The people were preparing to go into the Promised Land, and the time had finally come to divide up the land.

But one family had a problem. Zelophehad was a man with five daughters and no sons, and he had died in the wilderness before the Israelites reached the Promised Land. The rule was that when a father died, his money and land went to his sons. But because Zelophehad had no sons, the rulers ignored Zelophehad's daughters. It was like waiting in a long line for your turn to ride the best roller coaster only to be pushed aside so someone else could ride instead. It wasn't fair.

So Mahlah, Noah, Hoglah, Milcah, and Tirzah (the five sisters) got brave. They marched in front of what might have been thousands of people camped around the tent where the elders assigned land. They walked up to the men in charge (including Moses) and explained, "Our father's name will die out because he had no sons!" Then they asked, "Give us land among our father's relatives."

Now, back then, women weren't normally allowed to just ask for rights. But Moses listened to them and asked the Lord for His opinion. And God agreed that the women deserved the land (God is fair like that). Because these five spoke up for what was right, the Israelites changed the rules to make sure daughters could claim their father's inheritance whenever the same type of situation happened again.

In a lot of cases, I think we have to work on being quieter because our mouths can get us into trouble (well, at least mine does!). But sometimes we actually need to speak up—like when we see someone being treated unfairly or hurt.

Back to Gracie's problem. I did a little research in some history books to find proof that what she had said about America's founding fathers was true. Then I made copies and walked with her to talk to her teacher about it after school. You know what? The teacher listened! She said she had never read that perspective before, and she gave Gracie her points back.

It might be hard to do, but we honor God when we speak up for the truth. Is there a situation in your life where you need God's help to be brave like Zelophehad's daughters and take a stand for what's right?

Jesus, help me know when it's time to speak up for what's right and to do it in love. Amen.

Saved by Grace

Joshua 2; 6:22-25

You Have been saved by
gRace because you believe.
You did Not save youRselves.
It was a gift fRom God.

EpHesiaNs 2:8

I KNEW IT WAS COMING. I had heard my parents talking for
weeks, and I could just feel that my whole life was about to
change. But when the real estate agent put the For Sale
sign in my yard, I knew it was only a matter of time.
I was going to have to move, and there was nothing I could do about it. My only choice was how I
was going to go: kicking and screaming or with a
positive attitude.

I wonder if Rahab felt the same way. She was
living in Jericho, but she knew things were about to
change. The way she chose to handle that change was
pretty awesome, although I wish I had known about her
when I was packing up my things. It would have made my
move a whole lot smoother.

Do you know somebody at school who knows everything that's going on? Like, if you need to find out what the theme for homecoming will be this year you always know that person will somehow have the information?

I think Rahab must have been that kind of person. She seemed to hear all the talk and neighborhood gossip going around. The people were scared. Rumor had it that there was a new God bigger and better than the ones worshipped in Jericho, and He was helping His people, the Israelites.

And there was more. Rahab had also heard how the Hebrew soldiers destroyed every town they entered and took over. It was like they were indestructible! People around Jericho were really scared that their town would be next.

Jericho had reason to be afraid. God had put a strong and faithful new leader named Joshua in charge of Israel. Joshua had sent two spies into Jericho to find out the best way to attack the city. The spies ended up at the home of Rahab, who lived on the city wall. When Rahab saw the spies at her door, she could have called for Jericho's soldiers. Instead, she had another idea. "Come in!" she called. Then she showed the spies where they could hide on the roof of her house.

Meanwhile, the king of Jericho got word that the spies had stopped at Rahab's house. So he sent her a message to hand over the spies. She told the messengers, "They did come here, but they left." To sound even more convincing, she added, "Go quickly! Maybe you can catch them!"

So the messengers ran off to catch the spies, who were actually still hiding on Rahab's roof. When it was safe, Rahab went up to talk to the spies. "I know the Lord has given this land to your people," she admitted. "Everyone living in this land is terribly afraid of you and your God!"

Rahab begged, "Please show kindness to my family just as I showed you kindness." Then she told them to go into the hill country and hide out for three days. "The king's men won't find you there. Then after the king's men return, you can go on your way," she explained.

The plan made good sense, and the spies made a deal with Rahab: "You are using a red rope to help us escape. When we come back to attack Jericho, tie the same rope in your window, and bring all your family inside the house. As long as they are in your house, we can keep them safe."

Rahab gladly agreed and helped the spies escape into the night through her window in the town wall.

And you know what? God's people did conquer Jericho in the coolest way ever. The walls came crashing down, and in the end, only Rahab and her family survived. They were safe inside the house with the red rope dangling from the window.

Rahab had to choose sides, and she chose to be on the side of the one, true God.

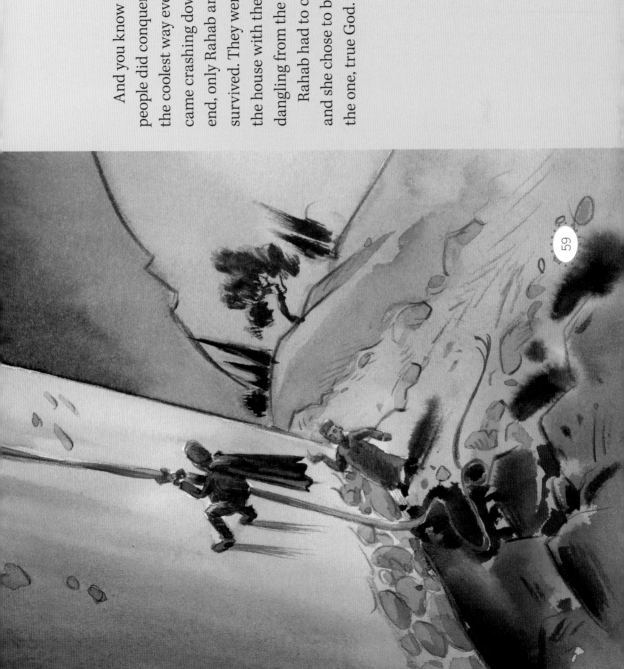

Now, I told you I wasn't excited at all about moving, and I'm sad to say I chose the kicking and screaming route. But I hadn't really heard about God yet, so I didn't see how this change could ever be good.

But after living here and hearing about who Jesus is, I've become more like Rahab. I've switched sides, and my attitude about change has, well, changed. Now I know God is in control and He works everything out for my good, even when I can't understand it.

You know what I know that Rahab didn't? In the list of Jesus' family history, guess whose name is there? Yep—Rahab's! She was faithful, and God's own Son was one of her descendents.

God, thank You for the grace You've shown me through Jesus. You love to save Your people! Amen.

Some trust in chariots, others in horses. But we trust the Lord our God.

Psalm 20:7

HOW WOULD YOU LIKE TO BE THE PRESIDENT? Yeah, me too. It'd be pretty cool. First thing I'd do is let girls play football, that's for sure. And then I'd get on to helping our country be an even better place to live. But when I think about being such a powerful leader, I can't help but think that will never be me. I've got dyslexia, for one thing, and sometimes it seems like that alone will keep me from doing anything great.

But I learned about this amazing woman in the Bible named Deborah. When Israel didn't have a king to lead them, God asked her to take over. Man, did she! She was a wife, a judge, and an army leader too. Whenever you doubt what God can do with you, just read about Deborah and remember that with God, our abilities have no limits.

The people of Israel weren't doing so well. In fact, they had forgotten about God and started doing everything wrong.

So God allowed Jabin, a king of Canaan, to attack Israel and defeat the people, making them slaves for the Canaanites.

King Jabin had a huge army with nine hundred iron chariots that was led by a cruel man named Sisera. He was so mean to the people of Israel that they remembered the Lord (finally!), and they called out to Him for help.

That was the first smart thing the Israelites had done in a long time. The other smart move was listening to Deborah, a female judge who loved and followed God. Day after day, Deborah would sit under a special palm tree that they actually named after her—the Palm Tree of Deborah—and she would listen to the Israelites' problems and make decisions about what to do. Everyone respected her opinion.

One day God told her to send a message to a man named Barak. She told him, "The Lord, the God of Israel, commands you: 'Go and gather ten thousand men. Lead them to Mount Tabor where I will make Sisera, the commander of Jabin's army, come to you. I will help you to defeat Sisera there.'"

Can you imagine? God had just given Barak the green light to defeat the awful people who had been treating his people so badly, and God promised to help him do it! Awesome. Barak must have felt powerful, right?

Nope. He was scared. So scared that he told Deborah, "I will only go if you will go with me." Unlike Barak, Deborah was brave and trusted God. She agreed to go, but she told Barak that he wouldn't get credit for the victory. Even though Barak had dragged his feet, God still fought for Israel and sent Sisera's huge army into mass confusion. In the end, Barak and Deborah won an incredible victory anyway, and Israel was saved.

I love Deborah's story, don't you? Deborah wasn't worried about the fact that a woman had never judged over Israel before. She followed God and filled the need at a time when Israel was desperate for some positive direction. She even obeyed when it meant riding into war against nine hundred iron chariots! And God made her a heroine.

Deborah's story reminds me that I don't need to get down on myself or give up on my dreams. After all, I serve the same God Deborah did. When He called her to do something, He gave her the ability to do it. And He promises to do the same for me and for you! Our weaknesses don't limit Him—they give Him a greater opportunity to show how powerful He is. And that makes our future full of hope!

Lord, I don't want to trust in my strengths or weaknesses. Help me trust in You and only You to make my life what You want it to be. Amen.

JAEL

Best Supporting Actress
Judges 4–5

You must choose for yourselves today. You must decide whom you will serve. . . . As for me and my family, we will serve the Lord.

Joshua 24:15

HOPE REALLY DID A GREAT JOB TELLING DEBORAH'S STORY. And Deborah deserves a lot of applause. But Hope didn't talk about one really important part of the story, and the perfectionist side of me can't let it go. Plus, it has a good message about how brave girls stay on God's side no matter what.

So I'm going to tell you. But beware: it's a little gross, and you might even find it hard to believe it comes from the Bible, but it does.

Right in the middle of Deborah's act of bravery, another woman stepped in to show just how far she'd go to stay on God's side. Her name is Jael, and the role she plays in Sisera's defeat is mind-blowing. Literally.

So, you already know the setup: Deborah and Barak went together to attack King Jabin and his iron army. But Deborah wasn't the woman who personally defeated Sisera. Jael was.

Jael's husband, Heber the Kenite, had made a peace treaty with bad guy King Jabin. But unlike her husband, Jael chose to be on Israel's side.

During the battle, Israel killed King Jabin's entire army except for its evil commander, Sisera, who fled from his chariot on foot—and ran fast and straight to Heber's house, where he thought he would be safe.

Jael welcomed him inside and pretended to care for him. "Please give me some water," Sisera asked. Thinking fast, Jael gave him some warm, soothing milk instead.

Maybe the milk—and all the fierce fighting—made Sisera sleepy because he was soon fast asleep, which was exactly what Jael wanted. She took a tent peg and—here comes the gross part (so stop reading if you're squeamish)—she hammered it through his head into the ground. Agghh!

But it worked. Evil Sisera died, and when Barak came over looking for Sisera, Jael showed him how the quick thinking of a God-fearing woman ended Israel's battle with a decisive victory.

I bet Heber, Jael's husband, thought he was making a smart decision becoming friends with King Jabin. After all, Jabin did have nine hundred chariots and a really big army. But Jael sided with the Israelites. She must have seen that no matter how big the enemy is, God is stronger still. And Israel was on God's side. So Jael chose to side with God's people.

Have you ever felt pressure from friends at school or in your neighborhood to go against what you know God wants? It can be so hard to do what's right and not follow the crowd.

That's why we can't leave out Jael's story (even if we don't want to think about the gross part). Her story reminds us how important it is to keep close to God, no matter what others do. God will make you brave if you ask Him, and His people always win in the end!

Lord, please give me faith to believe that You are stronger and better than anyone or anything in this world. Help me choose Your way today. Amen.

Tucked Under God's Wing

The Book of Ruth

"The Lord will reward you for all you have done. . . . You have come to Him as a little bird finds shelter under the wings of its mother."

Ruth 2:12

THE SUMMER MY PARENTS DIVORCED WAS A DARK, SAD PERIOD OF MY LIFE. I'm usually a very happy, positive person, but those hard times took the sparkle right out of my eyes. I felt like I was under a stormy cloud, and I couldn't find much to be happy about.

That's when I discovered Ruth's story in the Bible. Her tale starts off even worse than my summer did. But she kept on going. She looked up to God and His people for help. The more I read, the more I realized: God has a good plan in store, even though we may not see it at the moment.

By trusting God and staying with Him, Ruth got to be a part of an amazing love ____ was just the hope I needed because I could see that God was protecting ____ or me, just like He did for Ruth.

Life for Naomi had gone from bad to worse. A famine had forced her family away from their home to live in a foreign country. Then her husband died. Not long after that, her sons died too. Now Naomi had no husband or sons, and her sons' wives, Orpah and Ruth, were left as widows.

Naomi decided to go home to Bethlehem. So she told Orpah and Ruth to go back to their own homes and find a better life. Orpah kissed her and went on her way.

I don't know what Naomi had taught Ruth about the true God and His people, but it must have been good. Even though Ruth was from Moab, a place where the people worshipped other gods, she wanted to stay close to her mother-in-law—she wanted Naomi's God to be her God. They were family, and Ruth was home wherever Naomi was. "Every place you live, I will live," Ruth said. "Your people will be my people. Your God will be my God."

Ruth's decision was a big deal. Staying with Naomi meant leaving her parents and facing almost certain poverty since neither woman had any money. It even could have meant death. Ruth didn't care, as long as she and Naomi faced it together.

After a long, dusty journey back to Bethlehem, the two women were hungry. So Ruth suggested to Naomi, "Let me go to the fields. Maybe someone will be kind and let me gather the grain left behind in his field."

Ruth wandered into the field of Boaz, a very wealthy man who happened to be Naomi's relative. I can just imagine Boaz riding past his fields that day. When he noticed this foreign woman gathering the leftover wheat, he asked his servants about her and then called Ruth over.

"Listen," he told her. "Please stay here in my field to gather grain. When you are thirsty, you can take water from the jugs my servants have filled."

Ruth was amazed by his kindness. "Why are you being so kind to me? I'm just a stranger," she replied.

With great compassion, Boaz answered, "I know all about the help you have given to Naomi, even after your husband died. You left your father and mother and your own country and came to this nation where you didn't know anyone. The Lord will reward you for all you have done."

Boaz was right—God was definitely taking care of Ruth!

When Ruth returned home with an armload of grain and leftover lunch, Naomi was shocked. When she heard Boaz was behind it all, Naomi knew that God had been at work. "Our Lord continues to be kind to all people!" she exclaimed.

Ruth and Boaz were soon married. Ruth and Naomi had a safe, loving home to live in together, and they were amazed at how God's power had blessed them. Their lives had been full of death and loss, but God brought them to a better place than they could have ever dreamed.

Guess what happened next? Ruth and Boaz had a baby boy named Obed, and Naomi was happier than ever. Even better, Obed grew up to become the father of Jesse, and Jesse had a son named David—Israel's most famous king, known as the man after God's own heart. What a storybook ending for a real-life story!

Glory says . . .

Life can be a pretty awesome, beautiful thing. Watching the gorgeous fall leaves, seeing a garden of crazy-bright flowers, or spending an afternoon with your best friends can make you think that all's right with the world. But then the hard times come— like death, divorce, broken friendships, or whatever hurts our hearts—and suddenly it's hard to see the beauty. Everything looks so dark and hopeless. We start to wonder if God even cares.

Ruth reminds me that He does. God's stories in our lives never end on a bad note because He has something incredible planned for every one of His children. Like Ruth, we just have to keep hoping and trusting in God. I can't wait to see what He has planned for me—and for you too! Like little birds, He has us tucked right under His wing, where He loves us, protects us, and helps us grow closer to Him. Don't worry if you're tired or it's dark right now. The light will shine again, and you'll be ready to fly!

Lord, You are always taking care of me, even when life gets really hard. Thank You! Amen.

Hannah's Cry for Help

1 Samuel 1–2:11

While Jesus lived on earth, He prayed to God and asked God for help. He prayed with loud cries and tears to the One who could save Him from death. And His prayer was heard because He left it all up to God.

Hebrews 5:7

IT'S HARD BEING THE NEW KID. For starters, I'm not a big, light-up-the-room social queen. Plus, when I first moved to town it felt like everybody already had their friends and didn't need any more. I ended up feeling left out and just plain awkward.

So when I first moved here, I guess you could say I was stressed out. I felt like it was too hard to make a whole new group of friends when I was perfectly happy with the ones I had back where I used to live. I felt so sad that I didn't even want to see anyone or sing anymore.

I wish I had known back then about Hannah, one of my new favorite brave girls. She was in a pretty tough spot too because she felt forgotten and alone, just like me. But she knew to ask God for help, and He answered her giant request by giving her even more than what she asked for.

Hannah was already dreading it: the annual worship trip. Every year Elkanah and his two wives, Peninnah and Hannah, traveled from their home to Shiloh, the special place where they could offer sacrifices to God. Now, Peninnah and Hannah didn't get along so well. Back in those days, people believed that having children meant God liked you. Peninnah had lots of kids, but Hannah didn't have any. I bet Hannah felt pretty left out, a lot like I did when I first moved here.

Even worse, Peninnah wouldn't leave poor Hannah alone about not having children. Every time they went up to worship, Peninnah would tease Hannah and make her cry so hard that Hannah couldn't even eat. Elkanah tried to be a good husband and do whatever he could to comfort poor Hannah. "Are you sure you won't eat anything? Why are you sad?" he'd ask her. "Don't I mean more to you than ten sons?"

Elkanah loved Hannah, but he didn't understand her pain. It was too deep. But Hannah knew who did understand. She took all those years of heartache and went to the Tent of the Lord, the special worship place where God met with His people through the high priests. There, she poured out her heart to God. Tears streamed down her face as she silently prayed, mouthing the words without a sound coming from her lips. "Please, God, give me a son," she begged from her heart. "If You do, I will give him back to You to serve You always," she bargained. "Thank You for hearing my prayer."

At first, Eli, the high priest, thought Hannah was drunk because she was acting so weird. But when he realized she was praying, he added his own prayer, saying, "May God give you what you asked of Him." Suddenly, Hannah felt at peace. She knew God heard her prayer, and she felt better. She ate some food, and she was happy again!

Less than a year later, Hannah gave birth to a son and named
him Samuel. After he was old enough to eat solid food, Hannah
brought him to Eli so that Samuel could serve God in the Tent of the
Lord, just like she had promised. Samuel grew up to love God and led
Israel in God's ways all the days of his life.

I know that giving Samuel up to God must have been hard for
Hannah. But God blessed her obedience. He gave her many more
babies to raise, and every year she got to visit Samuel at worship. The
once dreaded trip was now Hannah's reason to sing!

Gracie says . . .

Now why didn't I think of that when I was having a meltdown about meeting new people? I could've taken my worries straight to God and asked Him for help like Hannah did.

I guess it's because I didn't know. I had no idea that God was someone I could talk to about my problems. Even now, I know there will probably be times when I forget, but God gave us His Word and other Christians to help remind us that He hears our prayers.

When I finally understood that God loves me and listens when I pray, I felt totally relieved—just like Hannah. And you know what? My smile came back too. And my voice. Soon I found myself singing again everywhere I went, and I'm sure God was listening.

Lord, thank You for knowing what I need and hearing me when I pray. You are so good! Amen.

Food for Thought
1 Samuel 25

> Wise people will receive honor. But foolish people will be disgraced.
>
> Proverbs 3:35

I HAVE ANOTHER BRAVE GIRL I WANT YOU TO MEET. And, of course, she was beautiful. And, of course, she was definitely not just another pretty face. Abigail, wife of Nabal, was as wise as she was lovely. Humble too. It was her quick thinking that saved her and her people from big-time trouble.

I can't say the same good things about her husband, Nabal, however. He was very rich, but his attitude was terrible. He thought he was more important than everybody else, and he treated people badly.

Anyway, I thought you should hear Abigail's story because she was so brave in the face of real danger—danger caused by her husband's bad decisions. Instead of getting mad at him, she just fixed the problem and let God handle her husband. She's a shining example of how beautiful a little humility and smart thinking can be.

t was sheep-shearing time in Carmel, and Nabal was busy shearing his three thousand sheep and one thousand goats. (That's enough wool for tons of great sweaters!) He had more than enough wool to share, but he didn't because he chose to be cruel and mean instead.

Meanwhile, David (you know, the famous one who killed Goliath?) and some of his men were living in a desert nearby. (He wasn't king yet, but he did have a lot of followers.) David knew about Nabal because when his shepherds had been among his men, David made sure that no one harmed Nabal's sheep. But now David needed a favor in return. So he sent ten of his men to Nabal to ask for some supplies.

Seems reasonable, doesn't it? But Nabal wasn't a reasonable man. Instead, he insulted the messengers and sent them back empty-handed. Well, when the messengers told David what Nabal said, David and four hundred of his men grabbed their swords, and it looked like a world war (Hebrew style) was about to start. "We'll just kill Nabal and everyone with him!" David and his men decided.

That's where Abigail stepped in. One of Nabal's servants ran to tell
her what a dumb thing her husband had done. Quickly, she packed all
sorts of yummy treats, loaded up several donkeys with all the goods,
and traveled straight to David. When she reached him, she bowed
before him. "Please don't pay any attention to my foolish husband,"
she explained. "We all know what a great person you are, and we are
so thankful for all you've done for us," she continued. "You wouldn't
want to ruin your great reputation by killing all of us, would you?"

Then Abigail offered David all the treats she had brought. Her
combination of repentance, compliments, and gifts won David's
heart. "You are a wise and blessed woman!" he said. "If you had not
met me, all of Nabal's men would've been dead tomorrow. Don't
worry, your people are now safe."

God, however, punished Nabal. The next morning, Nabal came home after a fun night at the king's banquet, and Abigail told him how close he had come to being killed. The Bible says the news actually turned his heart *into stone*, and ten days later, God caused Nabal to die.

As for Abigail? David came back and asked her to marry him. Wise woman that she was, she said yes!

Glory says . . .

Nabal was quite a doofus, right? When I heard that story, I wondered how he could be so selfish and foolish.

And then I started thinking about the other night, right after youth group. All the girls were still standing around talking when our leader came up to me and asked me to help clean up. But I wanted to keep talking. The more I thought about it, the madder I got. Why did she single me out to clean? Didn't she see I had more important things to do? And just when I was about to say something ugly, God reminded me of the differ-  ence between Nabal and Abigail.

Nabal didn't think before he spoke. And what he did think was self-centered and wrong—just like I was being at that moment in youth group. I stopped and said a quick silent prayer to tell God I was sorry, and then I got to cleaning. Soon everybody else joined in too, and we had fun cleaning together. It felt so much better to be wise and kind—like Abigail.

FatHeR, please Help me cHoose my woRds wisely so tHat I always HoNoR You. AmeN.

Treasure Hunt

1 Kings 10:1-13

> Cry out for wisdom. Beg for understanding. Search for it as you would for silver. Hunt for it like hidden treasure.
>
> Proverbs 2:3-4

IF YOU WENT ON A TREASURE HUNT, WHAT WOULD YOU EXPECT TO FIND? It would probably depend on what you think "treasure" is. Normally, we think of gold or diamonds or something. But really, it's whatever we think is important. For Glory, I bet "treasure" means those super-cute boots she found on sale. Hope might think it's her trophies. Gracie treasures the playlists of her favorite songs. And Faith really values a list with everything checked off.

Me? I think if you'd asked me a year ago, I would have said that I treasured being smart. I thought the best way to spend my time was reading and learning things to increase my IQ. But now, I'm thinking a little differently, thanks to the queen of Sheba—one of the most intelligent, brave Bible girls around. She already had money, power, fame, and probably the best education possible. In fact, she was smart enough to realize she was missing something more important than anything she already owned. Rumor had it that real wisdom, the kind that comes from God, could be found far away in King Solomon's palace. So that's where she went.

She was known as the queen of the South. As the ruler of Sheba, a country in southern Arabia (where Yemen is today), she had everything you'd think a beautiful, wealthy, and noble queen would need. But she knew better. She had heard that Solomon, King of Israel, possessed a treasure she didn't have—wisdom about God. She was willing to travel the 1,500 miles from her country to his just to find it. The queen had her servants load up her camels with gold, jewels, and more spices than you can imagine, and then the whole caravan headed for King Solomon's courts. After all, what price is too high to pay for real wisdom? How far is too far to go?

When she finally arrived at King Solomon's palace, the queen asked him every question imaginable—not to increase her IQ, but to test Solomon to see if everything she heard about his great wisdom was true. When she heard Solomon's wise answers and saw his blessed kingdom, the queen realized everything she had heard about Solomon was true. Not only did she see storehouses filled with gold and tables overflowing with the best foods, but also she saw Solomon's people all happy and healthy under his leadership. It was obvious in every way that Solomon was indeed wise and knew the secrets to being a great ruler.

The queen told Solomon she wanted to rule her kingdom as wisely as Solomon ruled his. As he explained the truth to her, the queen of Sheba worshipped God and said, "The Lord has given you incredible understanding about God and the right way to rule His people. My long trip was well worth the effort because what I've seen here is even better than the good reports I had heard. Praise the Lord your God!"

Truth is, God has given us lots of fun, neat stuff on earth and lots of exciting things to learn about. He wants us to enjoy what He's made. But nothing on earth even begins to compare with having a real friendship with Him. He is the greatest treasure we can ever find because His love for us lasts forever.

The queen of Sheba was rewarded in her search to gain the wisdom about life and God that she needed. What about you? Where can you go to find the world's greatest treasure? Fortunately, you and I don't have to load up any camels like the queen did (although I'd love to have one as a pet!). We don't even have to leave the house. We can just open up the Bible right where we are and find out all we need to know about God's love for us and His wisdom for our lives.

Lord, You have promised to reward us if we look for You. Help me turn to the Bible to find truth and wisdom because You are the greatest treasure. Amen.

A Captive Audience
2 Kings 5

You are young, but do not let anyone treat you as if you were not important. Be an example to show the believers how they should live. Show them with your words, with the way you live, with your love, with your faith, and with your pure life.

1 Timothy 4:12

I LIKE A GOOD PUZZLE AND LOVE TO FIGURE THINGS OUT. So last week my parents and I sat down at the kitchen table to plan the schedule for our church's upcoming Vacation Bible School. We were trying to decide how to organize all the teachers, rooms, and times so that lots and lots of kids would get to come. But after half an hour of trying, we still couldn't find an answer. We were getting really frustrated when my little sister, of all people, walked up to the table where we were talking. I didn't think she had been listening, but she put her hand up on my arm and matter-of-factly asked, "Why don't you just ask God about it? He'll tell you what to do."

Mom and Dad and I got really quiet because we realized my sister was showing a whole lot of smarts. Why hadn't we thought of that? My little sis totally reminded me of the servant girl in the story of Naaman. Naaman had a bad problem too and needed help. Just like my sister, his servant girl spoke up with an idea that saved the day.

First of all, you have to understand a little more about this special servant girl. She was from Israel and should have been with her parents. But the king of Aram had attacked Israel, and his soldiers had stolen many of the people to make them their slaves. This little girl was one of the people taken away from her family and home to serve the Arameans. But God never left her side, and she didn't forget Him either as she served Naaman's wife.

Who was Naaman? He was the commander of the army that had attacked Israel. So when Naaman came down with leprosy, a horrible skin disease, the little girl could have said, "Serves you right, you big bully!" But she didn't. Maybe she understood that God is always in charge, and she wanted to honor Him. So she told Naaman's wife about Elisha, the man of God in Israel who could heal Naaman.

The wife told Naaman, and Naaman told the king what this little girl said. Can you believe that her words influenced a commander and king? Well, they did. And Naaman traveled to Samaria for Elisha's help.

Elisha sent a message through his servants, and he instructed Naaman to bathe in the Jordan River seven times to become clean. Easy enough, right? But Naaman wasn't used to obeying orders. He liked calling the shots, and all that bathing sounded too, well, silly. His servants came to the rescue, urging him to be humble and obedient. Finally, Naaman listened, did what Elisha had told him to do, and was healed. Maybe Naaman realized he was a servant too—of the God who held Naaman's life in His hands!

Faith says . . .

What would have happened to Naaman if the servant girl had kept quiet? Most likely he would have lived for a long time with a horrible disease. Then he might have died from it. By speaking up, that little servant girl probably saved a man's life!

Do you ever feel like you are too young to have an impact in someone's life? The servant girl lets us know that age doesn't matter when God is with us. If He gives us a chance to tell others about Him so they can know Him better, then we need to be brave like the servant girl—and like my sister—and speak up. God is always with us, so our words have the power to bring hope to the people who hear them, no matter how young or old we are!

Lord, no matter how young I am, help me be brave and use my words to tell others all about You. Amen.

One Brave Beauty Queen
The Book of Esther

Charm is deceitful and beauty is passing, but a woman who fears the Lord, she shall be praised.

Proverbs 31:30 NKJV

WANNA KNOW WHAT I LOVE MORE THAN ANYTHING ELSE? God. But you know what else I really like? I'm almost afraid to say. Embarrassed, really. *Beauty pageants!* Yes, I have to admit. I loooove the drama, the shiny makeup, and the flowy, colorful dresses that sparkle in the spotlight.

You might not think that my two loves—God and beauty pageants—could possibly go together. But they can! You just need to meet Esther, one of my favorite brave—and beautiful—girls from the Bible.

I love Esther because she reminds me that God cares about all kinds of beauty. I think that's why He paints the morning skies with amazing sunrises, the green grass with colorful flowers, and the dark night with glittering lights. God shines His beauty throughout the whole universe!

And that's what I see in Esther's tale of bravery and hope. Esther entered the pageant of all beauty pageants—and won! Better still, God used her beauty—outward and inward—to save His people and show His glory in some amazing ways.

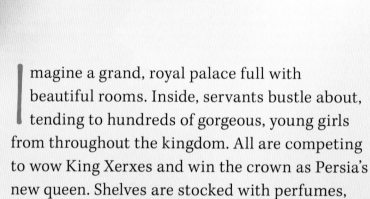

Imagine a grand, royal palace full with beautiful rooms. Inside, servants bustle about, tending to hundreds of gorgeous, young girls from throughout the kingdom. All are competing to wow King Xerxes and win the crown as Persia's new queen. Shelves are stocked with perfumes, powders, and every shade of eye shadow imaginable, just to make pretty girls prettier.

But not prettier than Esther. Esther glowed with a glory the other girls didn't have. Don't get the idea that life had always been easy for Esther. Both of her parents had died many years before. Her cousin, Mordecai, had raised her instead. He taught her how to love and trust God, even though they were Jews living under Persian rule.

Mordecai told Esther to keep her family information a secret. So she was powdered and primped like the other Persian girls for twelve long months. Then, after it was her turn to be taken before King Xerxes, he handed her the crown! Esther was the new queen of Persia!

Now, most fairy-tale stories would end right there with a "they lived happily ever after." But Esther's real-life story was not so easy. After she became queen, Cousin Mordecai sent word to her about an evil man named Haman, one of the king's top officials. Haman hated Mordecai and all the Jewish people. So Haman tricked the king into signing a law that said all the Jews needed to be killed.

You would think Esther could have marched right into the king's room and tattled on Haman, but she couldn't. First of all, the king didn't even know Esther was a Jew. Besides that, no one was allowed to go to the king without an invitation—not even his wife. If she tried but the king didn't want to see her, he could have her killed! Esther was afraid.

But Mordecai reminded her that God's ways are mysterious. Could it be that He had made Esther queen for the purpose of saving His people? Brave Esther chose to trust God. She sent a message to Mordecai: "Tell our people to pray and fast for three days. I will pray too. Then it is up to God. If I die, I die."

The three days passed. With her heart pounding and knees shaking, beautiful Esther arose and entered the king's court. And do you know what King Xerxes did? He invited Esther in! He wanted to see her. "What can I do for you?" he asked.

"You are invited to my special dinner feast!" Esther replied. The king was pleased. She also invited Haman. Haman thought he was pretty special, but he had no idea what kind of event Esther had planned.

The feast was such a success that the king and Haman eagerly agreed to come to another one Esther held. But during the second dinner party, she finally told King Xerxes the whole truth. "I am a Jew, and my cousin Mordecai who raised me is one too. This evil man, Haman, has tricked you into ordering that I, my friends, and my family be killed!"

King Xerxes got so angry! He immediately ordered Haman to be killed and the Jews to protect themselves against anyone who tried to harm them. God granted the Jews such an amazing victory that day that they still celebrate the Feast of Purim today in honor of the event.

Glory says . . .

Wow! Wasn't that an amazing story? You know, Esther could have been prideful. She was beautiful. Powerful. Famous. Rich. Everything most people think they need or want. She didn't have to risk her life the way she did.

But Esther had learned life's secret: God is a better reward than anything we can find on earth! Being queen and ruling the world was nothing compared to being faithful to God and a daughter of the King of kings! Esther chose wisely and won far more than a pageant. Her bravery won protection for her people and made the whole kingdom a better place.

Is there anything more beautiful than a heart that loves and obeys the Lord? I mean, lip gloss is great, but the way we look on the outside won't change people's lives. God shows us through Esther that real beauty comes by listening to God and living out what He says.

Lord, please make me beautifully bold like Esther so I can show the world how wonderful You are. Amen.

The Truth Keeper

2 Kings 22–23:1-3

Your word is like a lamp for my feet and a light for my way.

Psalm 119:105

I SHOULD HAVE KNOWN THEY'D PICK ME, THE NEW GIRL, TO WRITE ABOUT HULDAH. I mean, I'm still getting to know the more well-known women in the Bible—like Eve and Esther and Mary. So how on earth was I supposed to tell you about some woman named Huldah?

Well, I tell you what . . . when I started reading more about her in 2 Kings 22 and learning her story, I was totally floored. Huldah—the wife of a wardrobe keeper—was an amazing woman. Why hadn't I heard of her until now? I guess because I hadn't taken the time to read a lot of the Bible. Turns out, that was exactly the problem for the people of Judah. They had never read God's directions for them (they had actually *lost* the book!), and as a result, they were disobeying in some very horrible ways. But Huldah, who was also a prophetess (a woman who heard from and spoke the words of God), was there to set the record straight and prepare King Josiah.

By this time, Huldah was serving in the kingdom of Judah. The kingdom of Israel was split in two after Solomon's reign: Israel and Judah. Israel was in the north and Judah was in the south.

Judah was a total mess. Somehow along the way they had lost the Book of the Law that told them about God. The people had stopped following the Lord and were worshipping idols all over the place. But in walked Josiah, Judah's eight-year-old new king.

Many years later, Josiah ordered the people to repair God's temple. While they were cleaning, guess what they found? Yep—the Book of the Law! I bet they had to dust it off because they hadn't read it in forever. When they did, Josiah realized just how disobedient the people of Judah had been. *What should we do?* he wondered. He went to his high priest and scribes for help.

Hilkiah, the high priest, had heard about Huldah, a prophetess who always told the truth from God. Now Huldah must have been very respected to be known by such important people.

Hilkiah went to her and asked, "What's going to happen to our nation because we have sinned so much?"

Huldah answered bravely and honestly. "It's not good news for the people of Judah," she warned. "God is angry with them for forgetting Him and worshipping false gods, and He plans to punish them harshly because of it."

I'm just guessing, but it probably wasn't easy for Huldah to deliver such awful news. But because she knew God's truth and was brave enough to tell it, King Josiah was able to make changes and the Bible says he did what was right in the eyes of the Lord.

Huldah's story was a real eye-opener for me. I knew that God's Word was special and all, but I don't think I understood how important it was to read it for myself until I saw what happened to Judah. Those people were probably a lot like us, just living life like everybody around them did. After a while, they didn't even know when they were sinning because it seemed normal. Then they forgot God completely.

I don't ever want to make that mistake. I want to be sure that I stay close to the true God, and now I know I can only do that when I read what He has to say every day. I don't want to wake up one day and realize I've forgotten Him like the people of Judah did. I love that we can hear from Him like Huldah did by keeping close to His Word.

Lord, thank You for the Bible. It tells me who You are and how You want me to live. Amen.

More Than Enough

1 Kings 17:8-24

My God will use His wonderful riches in Christ Jesus to give you everything you need.

Philippians 4:19

A FEW YEARS BACK, MY PARENTS WERE READING IN THE BIBLE ABOUT HOW MUCH GOD CARES FOR THE ORPHANS. So they began praying, asking God how they could help. Next thing you know, we're working with an agency to help us adopt twin boys from the Ukraine.

The whole thing was a little scary, to tell the truth. We had a ton of paperwork to fill out, and my parents had to fly all the way across the world once before everything was finalized. At last, the twins were ready for adoption, and my parents let me come to the Ukraine with them to meet my new brothers and bring them home.

When we got to the orphanage, I was shocked. So many kids had no parents or a home! My parents could see that it bothered me, so they read 1 Kings 17 to me, and the story of the widow with Elijah gave me new hope.

The woman looked around and thought to herself that it just couldn't get any worse. First, her husband had died, leaving her and her young son to try to find enough work and food to live. But then a horrible famine came! Crops shriveled up, and so did the widow's hope. She had nothing left to feed her son or herself—just a little bit of flour and oil were left in the pantry, enough for one last meal. So she went out by the city gate to gather sticks for the fire (they didn't cook in ovens back then) when Elijah, a prophet, called out to her.

"Would you bring me a little water please?" he asked. As the widow went to get it, he added, "Please bring me a piece of bread too."

She stopped. She wanted to help, of course, but could she give away her family's last bite of bread?

"I barely have enough for my son and me to eat one last meal together," she answered sadly. "Don't be afraid," Elijah answered. Then he told her that God promised to keep her flour and oil jugs filled throughout the famine. The widow decided to trust God with the little that she had, so she made Elijah some bread.

Sure enough, when she went to make food for herself and her son, there was still plenty of flour and oil. And the next day, the same thing. And the next, and the next. God's plan rocked! She *never* ran out of flour and oil—He saved the widow, her son, and hungry Elijah, all at the same time!

But then tragedy struck in a new way. The widow's son grew sick and died. "God must be punishing me for my sins," she cried to Elijah. But the prophet knew God better. He carried the dead boy upstairs and prayed to God for healing. Suddenly, the boy began breathing again, and Elijah returned him to his mother. Wow!

After seeing God meet not just her family's need for food but also their need for life, she understood. "Now I know you really are a man from God and that the Lord truly speaks through you!" she exclaimed.

The widow finally got the picture: God is powerful, and He takes care of His people!

No matter how she looked at it, the widow believed her situation was hopeless. And it would have been, if God hadn't sent Elijah to the rescue. You see, she thought she and her son were suffering alone, but God was watching and planning to take care of them. Elijah obeyed God and went to the widow, and the widow trusted God by giving away what she thought was the last of her food. By looking to God for help, they both found that God was more than enough to meet all their needs.

And that's what gives me hope for the world's orphans. The same God cares for them and meets their needs—sometimes miraculously, but most often through His people. Whether we send money to the needy, write letters to encourage those who are suffering, or adopt kids like my parents did, we all can help show the world that God takes care of His kids!

God, thank You for all the ways You bless me. Help me share with others the way You have with me. Amen.

NEW TESTAMENT

His Love
Makes Us
Strong

Perfect Timing

Luke 1

Even when you are old, I will take care of you. . . . I made you and will take care of you. I will carry you, and I will save you.

Isaiah 46:4

AN AMAZING THING HAPPENED THIS YEAR. My apple tree was filled with a sweet crop of red apples—for the first time. That might not sound like a big deal, but ever since I was little, I have reeeaaaallly loved apples. My parents planted the tree for me years ago so that I could have some whenever I wanted them. But it took so long to grow. Some years it looked like nothing was happening at all. I thought about giving up on that tree altogether.

I wonder if that's how Elizabeth felt. She was married to Zechariah, a priest, and they really wanted to have kids. They prayed and probably begged God for one. But after many years passed and they both had grown very old, I'm sure they thought all hope was gone.

Even better than my apples, God had the sweetest surprise in store for Elizabeth. She just had to wait for God's perfect timing to taste the goodness. Boy, was it worth the wait!

Alarge crowd had gathered outside the temple. They were waiting for the priest to offer incense to God while they prayed. This year, Zechariah was chosen. He put on his special robes and walked inside.

I can imagine Zechariah looking around to make sure everything was in its place. Table of showbread? Check. The burning lampstand? Yep. The altar of incense? Right where it should be. Angel of God? WHAT? But there an angel was, giving old Zechariah a near heart attack!

Zechariah didn't know what to think. Fortunately, the angel knew just what to do.

"Zechariah, don't be afraid," he soothed. "Your prayer has been heard by God. Your wife, Elizabeth, is going to have a baby. A boy! You will name him John. You will be very happy. John will be a great man, and many people will be happy because of his birth."

Zechariah tried to take it all in. But even after the angel finished explaining how John was chosen to get the world ready for God's promised Messiah,

Zechariah doubted. "How can I know that you are telling me the truth?" Zechariah argued. "I am an old man! And my wife is old too!"

Wrong answer.

Turns out the angel was Gabriel, one of the angels closest to God, and he had come to deliver God's message personally. Zechariah's doubt didn't honor God, so the priest lost the ability to speak—at all—until John was born.

But Elizabeth got the message loud and clear when she became very much pregnant. She knew God had worked a miracle. Then one day her young relative Mary showed up at her door. Instantly, Elizabeth knew Mary was going to have a baby too—another miracle from God. Elizabeth cried out, "God has blessed you more than any other woman. You are the mother of my Lord, and here you are visiting me!" Elizabeth was astounded with just how good God was being to her. She said to Mary, "When I first heard your voice, the baby inside me jumped with joy. You are blessed because you believed what the Lord said to you would really happen."

But Elizabeth knew she was blessed too. Although her husband had doubted, God had still graciously answered their prayers in a way far beyond their dreams. And don't worry about old, quiet Zechariah. His speech returned after he obeyed God and wrote that his baby's name would be *John*.

Zechariah and Elizabeth grew even older together, filled with joy as John grew stronger and stronger in the Lord. In time, their baby boy became John the Baptist, the man who told Israel to repent of their sins because the Savior of the world was about to come for a visit! Now, wasn't all that worth the wait?

Honor says . . .

If anyone knows anything about being impatient, it's me. I mean, I even skipped a grade because I just couldn't get through school fast enough. I wanted to give up watering my apple tree because I thought it was hopeless and taking too long to grow. I always seem to be in a hurry. But why is it so hard to wait for something good to happen?

I tell myself to wait for God to answer my prayers, but then I get worried that He's not listening or I think I can handle the problem better by myself (wrong again!). I'm usually more like Zechariah, who prayed but didn't believe that God could actually still answer. I want to be more like Elizabeth and Mary, who honored God by believing His promise. If I will trust God to do what He says, I won't be in such a rush to do what I want without asking God's opinion. Instead, I'll wait for Him to show me which way to go.

Father, I know I can trust You to do what is best when it's time, so please help me wait on You.
Amen.

Yes to God

Luke 1-2; Matthew 1:18-25

I am not important, but God has shown his care for me, his servant girl.

Luke 1:48

I LOVE CHRISTMASTIME, DON'T YOU? I love the yummy food, the fun traditions, and the whole story of Jesus' birth. When I need to give someone an extra-special Christmas gift, I love to paint and frame a picture of the incredible star in the sky that night.

But I've noticed one problem with the Christmas scene we know so well. The story is so amazing that it almost seems like a dream or a fairy tale. When I stop to think about what actually happened, I realize it probably wasn't all warm and fuzzy like a Christmas card. How scary for an angel to appear out of the blue! And what would I have said if God told me I'd be the mother of the Son of God?

I'm afraid I wouldn't have been as brave as Mary. But her bold faith gave her the courage to trust the new plans God had given her.

I picture Mary in her cozy little house in Nazareth, her hometown. Maybe she was sweeping or cooking. The Bible doesn't say, but I bet she was thinking about Joseph, the man she was engaged to marry soon. Whatever she was up to, suddenly an angel of the Lord appeared to her, and said, "Greetings! The Lord has blessed you and is with you."

Well, as you can imagine, Mary was very confused and probably scared to death. It's not every day that God sends an angel to talk to you. But she didn't know the half of it yet. The angel comforted her, "Don't be afraid, Mary, because God is pleased with you!"

That must have been nice to hear. But then he told her the rest: "You are going to have a baby! You will give birth to a son, and you will name Him Jesus. He will be great, and people will call him the Son of the Most High. He will rule over God's people forever. His kingdom will never end."

With eyes wide, Mary gasped. "How is this going to happen?" she wondered out loud. Then the angel explained that God's Spirit would create His own Son inside her. She was going to be the mother of God's Son. While that information sank in, the angel said, "Elizabeth, your cousin, is very old. But she is also pregnant with a son. God can do everything!"

I don't know about you, but I think I would have fainted—first from the angel, then from the news. But Mary not only stayed steady, she said, "Yes!" and answered the angel with amazing faith and grace. "I am the servant girl of the Lord," Mary said. "Let this happen to me as you say!"

But it wasn't easy. Mary hurried over to Judea where she stayed with her cousin Elizabeth for a while. Then Mary had to tell Joseph that she was going to have a baby. When she did, he decided to quietly break off their engagement, but God sent an angel to Joseph too while he was asleep. The angel calmed Joseph's fears and assured him that the baby was from God and that He had a great plan for the child. So Joseph married Mary, and Mary's belly grew bigger and bigger.

So what's one of the last things you'd want to do when you were about to have a baby? Take a long, dusty trip to a busy town where you can't find a place to stay? Mary and Joseph had to do exactly that when they traveled to Bethlehem. The country's ruler, Caesar Augustus, wanted all the people to be counted in their hometown, and Joseph was from Bethlehem. That meant the city was overcrowded with all the other people who had come to register. Not a single room was available for the couple to rent for the night, but an innkeeper let them stay in his stable with his animals. It's a good thing, too, because Mary was ready to have the baby!

The only thing worse than traveling a bunch of miles when you're about to have a baby would be giving birth in a barn, out in the cold, but that's exactly what Mary did. She only had strips of cloth to wrap up baby Jesus. I bet she was wondering what God was doing. Then, when things couldn't get stranger, a bunch of shepherds showed up. They told the couple about these glorious angels who appeared in the night sky, announcing that the Savior had been born that day in Bethlehem. The shepherds wanted a closer look at this miracle baby announced by angels. In typical Mary style, she answered, "Yes."

Faith says . . .

When I was reading Mary's story, I couldn't help but think of my to-do lists. I'm such a planner, and I like to watch how everything I've planned falls into place. In a way, I feel like I'm in control of my life as long as things go the way I want. But what if God has a different plan for me? Will I be willing to listen and follow God like Mary, or will I insist on having my own way?

If I'm honest, I probably wouldn't show the same faith and obedience that Mary did. Not at first, anyway. But I really do want to have so much faith that I'd say yes to whatever God asks me to do. Like, if God asks me to make friends with the girl who's being picked on, I'll say yes. And if God wants me to tell my parents the truth even though I'll get in trouble, I'll say yes. If God asks me to cancel my slumber party plans when I find out that there will be a movie I shouldn't watch, then I'll say no to the party and yes to God! So lately, I've been praying before I even get out of bed in the morning. *God, how many ways can I say yes to You today?* Want to join me?

Lord, I want You to be in control of my life. Help me always say yes to whatever You ask. Amen.

ANNA

The Prize

Luke 2:36-38

Anyone who comes to God must believe that He is real and that He rewards those who truly want to find Him.

Hebrews 11:6

IF YOU LOOK IN MY ROOM, YOU'LL FIND A LOT OF DIFFERENT TROPHIES FROM ALL MY SPORTS ON THE SHELVES. But if you pick them up, you can see that they're really just blocks of wood with plastic pieces on top. They're not really worth anything other than the memories they bring me.

I started thinking the other day about how hard my friends and I work at school, sports, art—whatever it is we each spend time doing—just to get a prize that's not going to last. Most people in the world these days want to get rich and famous, drive nice cars, and have people notice them. Like my trophies, the money and fame make them feel like they've really accomplished something—but you know what? None of that lasts.

Anna's story in the Bible gives me a glimpse of something better. She spent her entire life on something that most people probably thought was a waste, but in the end she received a prize worth more than pure gold.

At first, Anna was probably like all the other young, married Hebrew girls her age. But something really sad happened. After being married only seven years, Anna's husband died. What was she going to do now?

Anna decided to dedicate her life to God and went to live in the temple where she served Him as a prophetess. For the next several decades, Anna worshipped there by fasting and praying to God and waiting for the Savior He had promised.

I don't know about you, but I think it would be hard to pray for an entire afternoon, let alone an entire lifetime. But Anna didn't stop because her focus was on God, and she knew He had made a promise and would keep it. Well, just imagine the day when Mary and Joseph took baby Jesus to the temple to dedicate Him to God. Wrinkled and gray, eighty-four-year-old Anna was probably going about her typical day of praying and worshipping when she looked over to see the newborn Savior! God had allowed her to see His promise really happen! Filled with thanks, she told everyone around her about Jesus, the Hope of the world.

Hope says . . .

Anna may have lost her husband at an early age, but she won the greatest prize of all by choosing to give her life to God. I mean, she got to see Jesus, Savior of the world, when He was still a tiny baby! What an awesome privilege to tell everyone else who had been waiting too that the time for hope had finally come!

You know, I spend a lot of time practicing for my sports, and a lot of time with my family, friends, and my schoolwork. But when it comes to reading the Bible and talking to God, I often cut it short or skip it altogether because I think I have better things to do first. But Anna reminds me that nothing in the world is more important than knowing God and worshipping Him. Her story proves how important prayer really is and shows how God loves to reward us when we follow Him.

God, the world tries to tell me that popularity and money and stuff are the most important things. Please help me remember that You are the greatest reward of all! Amen.

The Better Plan

Luke 10:38-42

God says, "Be quiet and know that I am God."

Psalm 46:10

GUESS WHO'S IN CHARGE OF THE YOUTH GROUP BACK-TO-SCHOOL BASH THIS YEAR? Yep, that would be me. And I'm so excited—I love party planning! We're supposed to be inviting friends and family who don't normally go to church, so it's kind of a big deal. And I want to make it bigger and better than ever before!

So my head is swimming with all the options. Should I choose a disco theme, with cool music and lots of lights? Or should I go with a beach theme and decorate with sea-shells and surfboards?

Before I drive myself crazy, maybe I should tell you the story of Martha and Mary, two sisters who had a big party at their house too. It would probably do me some good to slow down and remember what Jesus had to say about all their party plans and what was really important.

When Jesus was traveling through towns talking to people about God and His kingdom, He and His twelve disciples came to a country village called Bethany where two sisters named Martha and Mary lived. I imagine they were both pretty thrilled about Jesus coming because Martha invited Jesus to use her home as a place where He could teach. I bet both girls were really excited when He said yes. And maybe even a little nervous too. Not everybody liked what Jesus was saying. The Pharisees and other religious leaders of the day made life hard for anyone who supported Jesus. For these two girls to openly invite Him into their home meant that they didn't care what other people thought. They wanted to be as close as they could to Jesus. And now, the Messiah was coming to Martha's home!

So Martha most likely started doing what I've been doing: planning and preparing. When Jesus and all the other guests arrived (probably loads of them), lots of work needed to be done. So Martha got after it. I bet she was cleaning every nook and cranny and baking all kinds of goodies in the kitchen to serve everyone. *Wait. Where is my sister?* she wondered. Martha was tired of working so hard alone and wanted a little help. Then she realized her sister was not doing anything at all. She was sitting in the room where Jesus was and listening to Him teach!

Well, can you imagine how mad Martha got? She marched right into the room where Jesus was speaking and demanded, "Lord, don't you care that my sister has left me alone to do all the work? Tell her to help me!"

Whoa. Martha had gotten so busy with her plans and her work that she had forgotten *who* she was doing all the work for. Jesus gently reminded her by saying, "Martha, Martha, you are getting worried and upset about too many things. Only one thing is important. Mary has chosen the right thing, and it will never be taken away from her."

Glory says . . .

I am still excited about the back-to-school
bash (who doesn't love balloons and confetti?).
And I still want to make sure it is fun
and looks great for all the guests.
But Martha and Mary's story reminds
me that I don't need to go overboard on the stuff that
doesn't really matter. I mean, disco balls and funky
music are really cool, but they don't mean anything compared to knowing Jesus better.

So I'm praying already that God will bring
all sorts of new neighbors and friends over to
this year's party to hear about Jesus. But I'm
not going to worry about how great everybody
thinks the decorations and food are. I'm going to
relax, enjoy being with old and new friends, and pray that
God helps us all feel His love. After all, God says people will
know we are Christians by our love, not how well we can put on a party!

Lord, help me keep my plans focused on You!
Amen.

Healing Touch
Mark 5:24-34

"Come to me, all of you who are tired and have heavy loads. I will give you rest."

Matthew 11:28

ONE OF THE HARDEST PARTS OF BEING NEW IN TOWN WAS MAKING FRIENDS. It takes me a really long time to trust someone and let them really know me. When I moved here, I kind of felt lost and really alone. I didn't see how my situation was going to get any better, so I cried a lot.

But the pastor at my new church told the story about a woman Jesus healed in the Bible. She had been bleeding and hurting for twelve years! She didn't like her situation either, and she felt alone too since people didn't want to be around her because of her illness. But Jesus didn't see her that way. The way she trusted Him and the way He healed her was just what I needed to change the way I look at things.

Jesus and His disciples were swarmed on all sides by the desperate crowd who pressed in to see Him. Dust was thick in the air, and noisy conversation bounced all around Jesus as He walked and talked with the people.

The woman pressed into the crowd too. "If I can just touch Him, I can be healed," she told herself as she made her way nearer to Jesus. She knew she shouldn't even be there, among so many people. The poor woman had been sick and bleeding for twelve years, and no doctor could cure her. Because of her condition, she was called "unclean" and wasn't allowed to worship or visit with her family and friends. Her life seemed ruined.

But then she thought, *If I can just touch the hem of His robe, just the edge, I would be healed, and no one will even know.* So that's what she did. And she was instantly healed!

Only someone did know: Jesus.

"Who touched Me?" Jesus asked, looking at the huge crowd of people surrounding Him.

"Um, Lord, people are crowding up against You from all sides. Of course someone touched You," His disciples answered.

But Jesus was talking about the one who touched Him in faith. "Someone did touch me! I felt power go out from Me."

Shaking in fear, the woman bowed before Jesus and admitted what she had done. She, an unclean woman, had touched the Master! What would He think? Was this the end of her hope?

"Dear woman," Jesus answered kindly, "you are healed because you believed. Go in peace." And the woman walked away with her body and her heart healed by God's amazing power.

155

Gracie says . . .

That woman had a really big hurt, but she finally went to Jesus and found that He could do what all the doctors couldn't do. With one touch, He changed her whole life.

When I heard her story, I realized that Jesus could do the same thing for me—make me feel better. I knelt beside my bed one night and told God everything that was on my heart—how angry I'd been, how lonely I felt, and how tired I was of all that was going on. And you know what? God started something amazing that night. He showed me grace. Even though my attitude had been really bad, He made me feel loved. He filled me with a new sense of peace. And I knew that I could face all the new challenges in my life because He was with me. I knew it was going to be okay. And you know what? It is!

What problems do you have right now? Quit worrying and trying to fix them. Go to Jesus instead. He's the only one who can make you better.

God, You are the only One who can heal us when our bodies are sick and when our hearts are worried and sad. Thank You! Amen.

Living Water
John 4:1-42

"But whoever drinks the water I give will never be thirsty again. The water I give will become a spring of water flowing inside him. It will give him eternal life."

John 4:14

DID YOU KNOW THAT IF A THIRSTY ANIMAL TRIES TO STAY ALIVE BY DRINKING SALTWATER IT WILL DIE? The same is true for humans. I was just reading about it today at the library when I was researching how to help dehydrated animals. We've had almost no rain this summer, and I was hoping to find out some ways I could help the wild animals around here get what they need. I knew water was important, but I didn't realize how much drinking the wrong kind can hurt you!

Jesus had an interesting conversation about water one time with a woman who met him at a well in Samaria. Jesus gave her some life-giving information about how she needed an even better water source than that well. Then she turned around and shared the discovery with her whole town. Turns out a lot of the people had a dehydration problem, and the woman brought them to Jesus, who could satisfy their thirst.

The hot, midday sun was shining right over her head when the Samaritan woman came to draw water at Jacob's well as she did every day. But that day, she was surprised to see a Jewish man resting beside it. Even more surprising, He asked her for some water. Jews weren't supposed to even talk with lowly Samaritans, especially women.

Surely the man knows this? she must have thought.

The man said to her, "If you knew who I was when I spoke to you, you would have asked *Me* for a different kind of water—living water. And I would have given it to you."

Living water? Now the woman was really interested, but she wondered where on earth this man was going to get such a thing. "Sir, this well is really deep, and you don't even have a water jug. So where can You find living water?"

Jesus answered, "Every person who drinks water from a well will be thirsty again, but whoever drinks the water I give will never be thirsty again. The water I give will become a spring of water flowing inside him. It will give him eternal life."

Now, who wouldn't want water that made you live forever? So the woman replied, "Sir, give me this water so that I won't be thirsty or have to come draw water every day." She thought her days of hauling water and being thirsty were over. But Jesus was talking about her spiritual thirst. So He got a little more personal.

"Go get your husband and come back here," He told her.

"I don't have a husband," she stammered, uncertain where this conversation was going.

Then Jesus said, "You're right—you have no husband. You have had five husbands. But the man you live with now is not your husband."

Jaw on the floor! *How does this stranger know all these things about me?* she must have wondered. *Is He . . . a prophet? Is that how He knows all my secrets?* "You must be a prophet!" she said to Him.

No. Jesus was no prophet. "I am the promised Messiah," He admitted.

She was so excited that she left her water jug right there and ran back to town. "A man told me everything I've ever done!" she told everyone. "Come see Him. Maybe He really is the Christ!" So they did.

The rest is history. One woman's simple invitation led many in the town to Jesus, who gave Living Water to everyone who came to Him!

HONOR says . . .

The woman thought
she just needed some
water. Jesus knew she really needed God.
Searching for love in a bunch of bad relationships, she had come up empty and was dying of spiritual
thirst—until she met Jesus, the Living Water.

So what do you fill your life up with? Hanging out with friends?
Shopping? School? Although none of those are bad things, they can crowd
out the most important thing we need—a relationship with Jesus. If we start
with Him, then everything else we do will fall into the right place in our lives.
Think about how good it feels to drink a glass of ice water on a hot summer
day. Our relationship with Jesus does the same thing to our souls—it gives us
new strength and joy. Like the Samaritan woman, we can go out to everyone
we know and invite them to have a drink too!

Jesus, You're the only one who can meet my real
needs. Thank You for saving me with Your living
water! Amen.

Giving All You've Got

Mark 12:41-44

Each one should give, then, what he has decided in his heart to give. . . . God loves the person who gives happily.

2 Corinthians 9:7

LAST SATURDAY I EARNED SOME MONEY PULLING WEEDS FOR MY DAD. Well, I turned right around and took that money to the store to buy some sour straws, the best candy ever.

As I was relaxing back at home and gobbling them up, Caleb, one of my twin brothers, walked up. Of course he wanted one. So I gave him a red one, my least favorite. Then Josh appeared, wanting some too. I gave him another red. Then I pulled my bag away. "Enough, you two! These are mine!" I said, turning my back to them. I heard my mom yell from the kitchen, "Hope, please share with your brothers."

It was my candy! I earned it! And I had already given them each one. Why should I give anymore away? Well, the story of the widow with two coins had an answer. After my mom walked over and read it to me, those sour straws didn't taste nearly as good, and I was thinking about generosity (and candy) in a much different way.

One day Jesus was in the temple and sitting by the money-box where people came to put their donations. He watched several rich people come in and put large amounts of money in the box. I imagine anyone else watching would have been pretty impressed by how much those guys were giving to the temple.

But soon a widow came up to the box. She was obviously very poor, but she pulled out two small copper coins and put them in the box. They weren't even worth a penny.

Jesus was deeply touched. So He called His disciples over to show them what He saw.

"I tell you the truth," Jesus said. "This poor widow gave only two small coins. But she really gave more than all those rich people."

Then He explained what He meant. "The rich have plenty; they gave only what they did not need. This woman is very poor. But she gave all she had, and she needed that money to help her live."

Hope says . . .

I'm sure this news rocked the disciples' world. Along with all the other Jews, they probably thought the people who put the most money in the box were the most generous givers. But Jesus was not looking at their dollar amount. He was looking at

their hearts. What the rich people gave didn't cost them anything; they had plenty more left in their pockets. But what the poor widow gave cost her everything. God was pleased with her because she held nothing back from Him. I guess she believed that even if she gave it all away, God would still take care of her.

So as I looked back down at my wonderful sour straws, I realized I was just like those rich people. I had plenty, and I only gave what I didn't like or need. I had missed a chance to be like the widow and a chance to love others the way Jesus does. So I called Caleb and Josh back over and handed them the bag. "You guys split it up," I said and smiled. It was a moment sweeter than my candy!

LoRd, I don't want to Hold anything back from You. Please give me a generous HeaRt. Amen.

One Glorious Day

Luke 23:50-24:43; John 20:1-18

CRYING may last for a night. But joy comes in the morning.

Psalm 30:5

HAVE YOU EVER HAD SOMEONE OR SOME PET THAT YOU LOVED DIE? It's the worst. I remember when my Aunt Sarah passed away. I was pretty young at the time, so I didn't understand everything going on, but I knew that everyone, including me, was sad. She was my mom's sister and best friend, and we were shocked when it happened. It was the first time I saw how real death was, and there was nothing anybody could do to change it.

I imagine that's probably how the women who loved Jesus felt after He died on the cross. All they could do was go to His tomb and cry their eyes out.

But just when they thought all hope was lost, something spectacular happened that changed everything! Their tears of sadness became tears of joy when Jesus showed up alive. It's a story of hope coming alive on that amazing day!

Their hearts were aching as they looked up at Jesus, hanging dead on the cross. Then the women watched Joseph of Arimathea take His body down and carefully lay it in the cave-like tomb. Mary Magdalene, Mary the mother of James, Joanna, and some other friends believed Jesus' life was over. All they could do now was make spices for the body, but even that would have to wait until after the Sabbath was over.

Before sunrise of the new week, Mary Magdalene and the other women gathered their spices and were first to the tomb. To their horror, the huge stone guarding it had been rolled away! *Someone has stolen Jesus!* they thought. So Mary ran to tell Peter and John the bad news. They all ran back to the tomb and saw the same scene: an empty tomb with only Jesus' burial clothes lying inside. What had been terrible had gotten even worse! Then they left, sad and scared. But Mary stayed, sobbing outside the tomb.

Suddenly, two angels appeared in the tomb and asked Mary, "Why are you crying?" Choking back her tears, she explained, "They have taken my Lord. I don't know where they've put Him."

Then another voice sounded behind her. She turned and saw a man she thought was the gardener. "Did you take Him away, sir? Tell me where you put Him, and I will get Him."

Then Jesus called to her by name, "Mary!" She instantly recognized His voice and realized who He was. "Teacher!" she shouted in total surprise and excitement. I cannot even imagine the shock and joy she must have felt at that moment. He told her to go tell everyone what she'd seen.

She flew like the wind to tell the disciples. "He's alive! The Lord's alive!"

But guess what? No one believed her. The story was too unbelievable! Just too crazy, it seemed, until Jesus appeared to the other disciples too. Then He showed up in Emmaus, and He appeared to His disciples again and ate fish with them. Jesus really was alive! Now that's what I call an amazing comeback. And He brought back all the hope and joy our world needs on that incredible day!

Glory says . . .

I love how Jesus turned the women's sadness into celebration, don't you? I want to read it over and over again because even though it sounds too good to be true, it really happened! Jesus did what no one else could do. He defeated death! And because He did, we can celebrate instead of being sad. Even though death seems like the end, it isn't. Jesus died for us so that we can live forever with Him.

Although it's sad for us when we lose people we love, like my Aunt Sarah, we can know it's not the end, thanks to Jesus. Aunt Sarah loved God, and I know she's in heaven now, enjoying a never-ending, perfectly happy life with Jesus. One day I'll get to go there too! And there's nothing more awesome than that.

Jesus, only You can change such sadness into pure happiness. Thank You for giving me the chance to live with You forever! Amen.

The Power of Prayer

Acts 12:1-16

The LORD has heard my cry for help. The LORD will answer my prayer.

Psalm 6:9

THIS YEAR I DECIDED TO BE BRAVE AND TRY OUT FOR A SOLO IN OUR CHOIR'S SPRING PRODUCTION. I was soooo nervous, and I asked my parents and all my friends at youth group to pray. I just wanted to do my best and not make a fool out of myself.

When the director posted the decisions on the wall outside the choir room, I almost couldn't look. But there it was—my name, beside the song I wanted to sing! Even though I had everybody praying, I didn't really think God was going to answer like that.

I imagine Rhoda must have felt the same way, only she and all the other Christians were praying for something a lot more important than a solo. They were praying for Peter's life. When Rhoda got to see God's answer before anyone else, she was as surprised as anyone.

Everyone knew it was a terrible situation. King Herod had just killed James (the brother of John), and now he had Peter in prison too. If Peter didn't get out of there, he'd be dead next.

So all the believers gathered together at Mary's house. (I know there are a ton of Marys in the Bible. This one is John Mark's mom.) All night long, they prayed together for a miracle for Peter.

Little did they know that *while* they were praying, God was acting. He sent an angel who appeared right in the middle of Peter's cell while he was sleeping. The angel shook Peter awake. "Hurry! Get up!" he urged as Peter's chains simply fell off. "Get dressed and follow me!" the angel commanded. He led Peter past all the prison guards to a safe place outside. Then Peter headed straight to the house where he knew his friends were praying.

Now, I love this part. Peter knocked on the door, and Rhoda, the servant girl, answered. When he said, "It's me, Peter," she got so excited that she left him standing outside while she ran to tell the others. Although they didn't believe her at first, she eventually convinced everyone to come to the door. Finally, they opened it! It *was* Peter, alive and well. God had answered their prayers.

Gracie says . . .

I don't know why I have a hard time believing that God listens to me when I pray, but apparently it's a problem a lot of God's people have. I guess because we can't see Him with our eyes, we figure He can't hear with His ears. But Rhoda's story tells me He does.

My own story about the solo part tells me He does too. In fact, if I think about it, I can think of all sorts of prayers God has answered for me and my friends. Can you?

One way for me to remember is to write down all the things I've prayed about. Then when God answers, I write down how He did it, with the date. When I look back over the pages, I have a history book of how God has been faithful to me! So the next time I start to doubt God is listening, I look back on all He's done and I remember: God has the power to do anything, and He listens when we pray!

God, You are awesome because You listen to our prayers and answer them. Thank You! Amen.

Growing Faith

Acts 16:13-15, 40

So the one who plants is not important, and the one who waters is not important. Only God is important, because He is the One who makes things grow.

1 Corinthians 3:7

BEING HOMESCHOOLED, I DON'T GET TO SEE TONS OF FRIENDS AT SCHOOL EVERY DAY, SO WHEN A NEW FAMILY WITH A GIRL MY AGE MOVED IN NEXT DOOR, I WAS SO EXCITED! But after she and I had spent some time together, I realized she didn't know anything about Jesus. I asked my parents what I should do, and they told me just to show her God's love and tell her what I believed whenever she asked.

Wouldn't you know my friend started asking me questions the very next day? She asked why there were so many Bibles in our home and why we said a prayer before lunch. I couldn't believe it. God was giving me a chance to tell my new friend all about Him. It totally reminded me of the Bible story about Lydia, a lady who was ready to know the true God.

Paul and his buddies, Timothy and Silas, were in the middle of a major mission trip. They had already visited lots of different places looking for people who had never heard of Jesus so they could tell them all about Him. God's Spirit led them to the city of Philippi, one of the biggest cities in Macedonia. They had stayed there several days when it came time for the Sabbath (the Jewish day of worship held each week).

Paul decided to head to the river just outside the gates of town, hoping to find a special place for prayer. There he and his friends found a group of women already gathered. One of them was a special woman named Lydia. A businesswoman, she was known for the expensive purple cloth she sold. From what I understand, only really wealthy people could afford her kind of fabric, so she probably knew a lot of interesting people.

But the most important person Lydia knew was God. Even though she didn't know about Jesus, she had heard about God and worshipped Him as best she could. The ladies agreed to let Paul speak to their group. And while Lydia was listening to the gospel, God changed her heart and allowed her to believe what Paul was saying.

Lydia was so excited to finally know the part about God's story she had always been missing! She immediately went home and told her family, and before you know it, she asked Paul to baptize her and her entire family, who also believed! Because she was thankful for Paul and his ministry, Lydia invited the men to stay in her home while they were preaching in the city. Even after they escaped from prison a little while later, they went straight back to Lydia's place, where they knew they'd always be welcomed because of what God had done in her heart.

God knew about Lydia long before Paul did. So God arranged for Paul to meet Lydia at just the right time and to tell her all the information about Jesus that she had been missing. Isn't it amazing how God uses His people to spread the Good News about Jesus?

Even more amazing—God used me too! I was able to tell my new friend why Jesus was so important to me and my family. As she listened, I could tell she was thinking. She said, "I never heard anybody talk about God like that. Can I come to church with you sometime and learn more?"

Wow. I realized that I don't have to be nervous about sharing my faith or force someone to talk with me about Jesus. When I meet someone like Lydia or my neighbor, all I have to do is tell them all why I love Jesus. God does the rest.

Father, show me the people in my life who need to hear Your Good News. Amen.

My children, our love should not be only words and talk. Our love must be true love. And we should show that love by what we do.

1 John 3:18

ONE SATURDAY A MONTH, MY FAMILY AND I GO DOWN TO THE CITY WHERE OUR CHURCH HAS OPENED A SOUP KITCHEN AND CLOTHES PANTRY. It's kind of like a little cafeteria and clothing store where poor people can come get a hot meal and pick out some clothes for their families without having to pay for them. My brothers and I actually like going because we've gotten to know some of the families that come and it's cool to be able to help out. Last week one of the older men came up to me and said, "Hope, you all are doing a good thing here. I'm really grateful for what you do for my family." I was so amazed! I didn't realize that our Saturday trips were helping these people that much.

It reminded me of the Bible story about Tabitha. She loved to do good things for others. She had touched so many people that when she died, they begged for Peter to come and help. And wow, did he! Her amazing story helps me remember how important it is not just to say I love God—but to show it.

Tabitha (who was also known as Dorcas) was a follower of Jesus who loved to help the poor by sewing them nice coats and shirts. One day Tabitha got so sick she died! *Why would God take away our dear friend?* all the widows and poor people must have wondered. Then they remembered that Peter was staying in a town nearby. So the believers sent two men to get him.

Peter came immediately and went upstairs where all the widows were crying really hard. They were so sad! "Peter, have you seen these clothes Tabitha made?" they asked, holding her creations in front of them. Memories of her and the work she left behind were all they thought they had left.

Then Peter told everyone to leave. Kneeling down beside Tabitha, Peter prayed. Then he looked at her body and said, "Tabitha, stand up!" And she got up!

Oh my goodness! Just like Lazarus,
Tabitha rose from the dead! You know
that the word got around town fast
because everyone knew who Tabitha
was. Now everyone knew what kind of
God she served!

Everybody missed Tabitha when she died because she had helped them so much. Even though she was just one single girl, God had used her to help so many.

As I thought about what the old man from the soup kitchen said to me, I realized God was using me. It didn't matter if I had dyslexia or if I was just a kid. God could use little old me to change other people's lives! Tabitha's story shows it's true. It also shows that real love for God proves itself through action. It's just like this: I can say I'm a soccer player all day. But if I don't ever dribble a ball or shoot a goal, I'm just all talk. It's not real.

I don't want to just say I love God. I want to *show* how much I love Him by doing the things that matter to Him, like helping the poor. I'm so glad that God can use me like He did Tabitha, not just one Saturday a month, but a little bit every day to bring some hope to everyone around me.

Lord, please use me to help others and bring Your hope to their lives. Amen.

Parental Guidance Suggested

2 Timothy 1:3-7

My child, listen to your father's teaching. And do not forget your mother's advice. Their teaching will beautify your life. It will be like flowers in your hair or a chain around your neck.

Proverbs 1:8-9

LAST WEEK I FOUND MYSELF IN A TOUGH SITUATION. I was in the locker room changing into my P.E. clothes when the girls next to me started giggling, turned to me, and asked, "Did you see how fat Lexie has gotten?" Lexie's back was facing us, and she didn't hear them.

I froze. The cool, popular girls were talking to me! But they wanted me to say bad things about someone else. Suddenly, some of my mom's advice about avoiding gossip popped into my head, and I knew what I should do.

In a weird way, that day makes me think of Timothy—a young man training to travel with Paul and tell people about Jesus. Even back then, trying to please God could be hard. But Paul encouraged Timothy to think about what his mom, Eunice, and grandma, Lois, had always taught him. Because those two women taught him the truth, Timothy could stay strong and make the right decisions.

The Bible doesn't go into a lot of detail about Timothy's family. We do know that Lois (his grandmother) was the first of the group to put her faith in Jesus. But she didn't keep it to herself. She most likely shared it with her daughter Eunice because Eunice and Lois taught Timothy all about Jesus. By the time he was a young man, Timothy was helping Paul take the gospel to the world.

But here's where the story starts to sound like mine: Timothy knew what to do because he had learned what was right when he was younger. But Paul wanted to make sure that Timothy would remember all he had learned and not be afraid to share it. So Paul reminded his young friend about the kind of real faith Timothy's mom and grandma had shown him through the way they lived. When he remembered how well they showed their love for Jesus, he knew he could be brave and live for God like they did.

Honor says . . .

Imagine what would have happened if Lois and Eunice hadn't bothered to tell Timothy about Jesus! He wouldn't have been ready for Paul, and tons of people would have missed out on the gospel.

If you're like me, you proba-bly never think about how great it is that we have parents and teachers like Lois and Eunice who care enough to teach us about Jesus and the Bible. But they really are a big gift from God. We should thank these special people and, like Timothy, remember the good things they've taught us.

As for my P.E. situation, I really wanted those popular girls to accept me, but my mom had taught me that it's more important to honor God with my words than to fit in. I just gave those girls a look… you know, that look your mom gives you when she's not mad but she doesn't approve? Anyway, it worked. They quit talking about Lexie and left the locker room. And I felt a little braver, like I had the same spirit in me that Lois and Eunice had. Which, of course, I do, thanks to Jesus!

Lord, thank You for giving me leaders to teach me about You. Help me remember their good lessons. Amen.

How to Be Brave
Acts 18; Romans 16:3; 1 Corinthians 16:19

Jesus said to the followers, "Go everywhere in the world. Tell the Good News to everyone."

Mark 16:15

I THINK ACTS IS BECOMING MY FAVORITE BOOK IN THE WHOLE BIBLE. It's filled with brave girls and guys who risked everything to tell the world about Jesus. I know because I read it last week when I was looking for a boost of courage and one of my friends from youth group told me to read it. Some friends from choir had signed me up to sing at the county fair! I was so excited about the chance to sing in front of so many people, but then I got really nervous. Not just because of the singing, but because I knew lots of my friends from school would be there. What would they think about me singing a song about Jesus?

So I was glad when I came across the story of Priscilla and her husband, Aquila, a couple who served Jesus even when it was hard. They risked their home. Their safety. Their jobs. But it didn't matter to them because God was most important. Their story reminds me that there's nothing in this world worth holding onto except Jesus. And His love makes us brave like Priscilla and makes us want to follow God no matter what.

riscilla and her husband, Aquila, were Christian Jews living in Corinth because Rome's ruler, Claudius, had booted all the Christians out of his city. Paul decided to come to Corinth during one of his mission trips, and he stayed with and worked with Priscilla and Aquila while they made tents for a living.

God told Paul to stay in Corinth for a while because a lot of people in that city needed to learn about Him. So Paul obeyed and taught the people for over a year and a half, even though it was very dangerous there to preach the gospel. Priscilla and Aquila risked their own lives to protect Paul while he preached. They must have learned so much from Paul because when he decided it was time to leave and go to another land, they went with him. Priscilla became one of the first women missionaries!

In the city of Ephesus, Priscilla and Aquila met a Jew named Apollos who was teaching about the Lord in a way that really made the Jews think and listen. But Apollos didn't have all the details about Jesus, so Priscilla and Aquila invited Apollos to come visit them, and they taught him the full truth. Apollos became an even better speaker for Jesus, all because Priscilla and her husband were willing to risk it all and share the Good News.

Gracie says . . .

I guess by now you know I don't like change very much. But I'm also learning that God doesn't always let us stay where we are. He wanted me to be brave and do something that scared me—singing in front of all those people at the fair—so that others could hear about Him. So that's what I did!

I wonder if Priscilla was ever scared. She had already left Rome, her home, and then Corinth where her friends from church still lived. And she had to speak out about God in a time when it was really dangerous to do so. God must've made Priscilla brave too.

What about you? Are you able to talk to your friends about the great things God has done for you? Has God shown you someone new who needs to know about Him? Believe me, I know it's scary. But if we're on God's side, why should we ever be afraid? Let's pray together that God will help all of us be brave and tell everybody about Him!

Jesus, please help me bravely share the Good News about You! Amen.

Which Brave Girl Are You Most Like?

Which accessory can you not live without?

   a. flip-flops because they're so comfy
   b. super-cute headbands—the more sparkles, the better!
   c. a ponytail holder—you always have one on your wrist
   d. a yellow T-shirt is always a classic choice
   e. glasses—you're as blind as a bat without them!

If someone spilled open your backpack or purse, which item would most likely be inside?

   a. headphones, so you can listen to your favorite tunes on the go
   b. a lot of stuff—all covered in glitter and rhinestones for extra glam
   c. a football—you never know where the perfect game might happen!
   d. a paint brush to add color to your masterpiece
   e. a mountain of books! People often ask you if you're carrying a
      bag of bricks

What's your favorite go-to outfit?

   a. nice and breezy summer dresses
   b. pink skirts go with everything, right?
   c. jerseys show your spirit for all of your favorite teams!
   d. overalls are super comfy and casual
   e. a nice green jumper is perfect for school or church

How would you feel about playing a game of football?

a. I wouldn't mind it much—can I still wear my flip-flops?
b. Um, I think I'll pass.
c. Sign me up! I call QB!
d. That could be fun. But what if I get grass stains on my overalls? Or drop the ball? Or I break a bone??
e. The guys would probably think I'm super cool. I'm in!

If you had to do a history project on a famous person, who would you choose?

a. Taylor Swift
b. Audrey Hepburn
c. Serena Williams
d. Georgia O'Keefe
e. Marie Curie

Which accomplishment would you be most proud of?

a. your first solo at church
b. being elected president of the school beautification club
c. winning first place in the city softball league
d. your first oil painting
e. earning an A+ in science

If you could go on vacation anywhere, where would you go?

a. back to your hometown to see all of your old friends and hangouts
b. the Amazon Rainforest to see God's most beautiful creations and creatures
c. the National Baseball Hall of Fame

d. the Metropolitan Museum of Art in New York City

e. the San Diego Zoo

How do you most like to wear your hair?

a. letting down your natural, bouncy curls

b. with a cute, colorful headband

c. in a short bob cut

d. just sleek and straight

e. in a beautiful braid

What would you most like to do on a summer day?

a. going for a ride on the swings (They will always be your favorite!)

b. hiking to see a beautiful waterfall

c. playing beach volleyball

d. lounging by the lake to paint a perfect picture

e. visiting a farm to go horseback riding

What is your favorite personality trait about yourself?

a. your beautiful signing voice

b. your impeccable fashion sense

c. your agile athletic abilities

d. your artistic eye

e. your amazing memory

What's your favorite snack?

a. cookies

b. cupcakes

c. popsicles

d. cheese and crackers

e. celery sticks

 If you answered mostly As, you're like Gracie— shy but sweet, and oh-so talented.

 If you answered mostly Bs, you're like Glory— appreciative of beauty inside and out.

 If you answered mostly Cs, you're like Hope— a girl who plays hard and loves everyone.

 If you answered mostly Ds, you're like Faith— thoughtful and artistic.

If you answered mostly Es, you're like Honor— smart and caring.

Brave Verses

God did not give us a spirit that makes us afraid. He
gave us a spirit of power and love and self-control.

2 TIMOTHY 1:7

"Remember that I commanded you to be strong and brave. So don't
be afraid. The Lord your God will be with you everywhere you go."

JOSHUA 1:9

Watch, stand fast in the faith, be brave, be strong.

1 CORINTHIANS 16:13 NKJV

Be strong and brave. Don't be afraid of them. Don't be frightened.
The Lord your God will go with you. He will not leave you or forget you.

DEUTERONOMY 31:6

You are of God, little children, and have overcome them, because
He who is in you is greater than he who is in the world.

1 JOHN 4:4 NKJV

"In this world you will have trouble. But be
brave! I have defeated the world!"

JOHN 16:33

Be strong. Let us fight bravely for our people and for the cities
of our God. The Lord will do what he decides is right.

2 SAMUEL 10:12

All you who put your hope in the Lord be strong and brave.

PSALMS 31:24

Finally, be strong in the Lord and in his great power. Wear the full armor of
God. Wear God's armor so that you can fight against the devil's evil tricks.

EPHESIANS 6:10–11

The Jewish leaders saw that Peter and John were not afraid
to speak. They understood that these men had no special
training or education. So they were amazed. Then they
realized that Peter and John had been with Jesus.

ACTS 4:13

Lord, we are your servants. Help us to speak your word without fear. Help us to be brave by showing us your power.

ACTS 4:29–30

We have this hope, so we are very brave.

2 CORINTHIANS 3:12

When I am afraid, I will trust you. I praise God for his word. I trust God. So I am not afraid. What can human beings do to me?

PSALMS 56:3–4

She is strong and respected by the people. She looks forward to the future with joy.

PROVERBS 31:25

Be strong and brave and wait for the Lord's help.

PSALM 27:14

I write to you ... because you are strong; the word of God lives in you, and you have defeated the Evil One.

1 JOHN 2:14

People will say bad things about you and hurt you. They will lie and say all kinds of evil things about you because you follow me. But when they do these things to you, you are happy. Rejoice and be glad. You have a great reward waiting for you in heaven. People did the same evil things to the prophets who lived before you.

MATTHEW 5:11–12

Be strong and brave. Don't be afraid or worried because of the king of Assyria or his large army. There is a greater power with us than with him. He only has men, but we have the Lord our God. He will help us. He will fight our battles.

2 CHRONICLES 32:7–8

Have courage. May the Lord be with those who do what is right.

2 CHRONICLES 19:11

Be strong and brave. Do the work. Don't be afraid or discouraged. The Lord God, my God, is with you. He will help you until all the work is finished. He will not leave you.

1 CHRONICLES 28:20

The people who trust in the Lord will become strong again.
They will be able to rise up as an eagle in the sky. They will run
without needing rest. They will walk without becoming tired.

ISAIAH 40:31

Be strong. Let us fight bravely for our people…
the Lord will do what he decides is right.

2 SAMUEL 10:12

It is God who arms me with strength.

PSALM 18:32 NKJV

Be strong. You must be careful to obey everything the Lord has commanded.

JOSHUA 23:6

She does her work with energy. Her arms are strong.

PROVERBS 31:17

Be Brave & Beautiful

With God's power working in us, God can do much, much more than anything we can ask or think of. To Him be glory!

Ephesians 3:20

So there you have it—a glimpse into the lives of some of the bravest Bible women of all time. Did you get fired up? We sure did! Learning about all of those amazing stories and knowing that the same God who worked their miracles lives inside us too . . . well, it's *incredible*.

Just think about it: God says He stays the same yesterday, today, and forever. If He was powerful enough in Bible days to part seas in half, heal the sick, and even raise the dead, why do we think He can't help us in the problems of our daily lives? Not only can he help us live stronger—He is also ready to work eternal, world-changing power through us when we make ourselves available to Him. He is more than able!

So we don't want to live ordinary, worry-filled, stressed-out lives. Instead, we want to be wise like Deborah and bold like Esther. We want to serve like Tabitha and worship like Mary. We want God—Maker of all the stars in the universe—to shine His power and glory through us in amazing ways too. All it takes is faith and an obedient heart, which God promises to give us if we just ask.

So what are you waiting for? Join us and ask God right now to make you bold for Him. Then watch in awe as God answers that prayer, changing each one of us into a Brave Girl of God.

Hope Glory Faith
gracie Honor

The Brave Girls

Brave Girls is a new brand from Tommy Nelson

that strives to pour the love and truth of God's Word into the lives of young girls, equipping them with the knowledge they need to grow into young women who are confident in Christ.

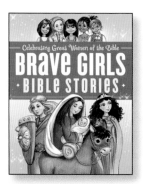

Brave Girls Bible Stories

Learn the Bible alongside the Brave Girls, who are just like you! Each devotion begins with an introduction from a Brave Girl, dives into a story about a brave (or not-so-brave) woman of the Bible, and closes with some insight from the Brave Girl character.

Brave Girls Devotionals: Better Than Perfect and Faithful Friends

The Brave Girls are back! These two 90-day devotionals let readers learn more about the lives of the Brave Girls and how they tackle important issues like being a good friend and knowing God loves you no matter what. Coming in Spring 2015!

Brave Girls Bible

This beautifully illustrated, two-color, expanded-content ICB study Bible features characters from the Brave Girls brand who are eager to teach readers about the Word of God and how they can apply the Bible to their everyday lives. Coming in Fall 2015!

9780529108982-A